JOURNEY OF THE SOUL SERIES

— Book 3 —

THE NATURE OF GOOD AND EVIL

ALSO BY SYLVIA BROWNE

BOOKS

Adventures of a Psychic (with Antoinette May)
Astrology Through a Psychic's Eyes
Blessings from the Other Side*
Life on the Other Side*
Meditations
The Other Side and Back (with Lindsay Harrison)*
and . . .
My Life with Sylvia Browne (by Sylvia's son, Chris Dufresne)

The *Journey of the Soul* Series

God, Creation, and Tools for Life (Book 1)
Soul's Perfection (Book 2)

AUDIOS

Angels and Spirit Guides
Healing Your Body, Mind, and Soul
Life on the Other Side (audio book)*
Making Contact with the Other Side
The Other Side of Life
Sylvia Browne's Tools for Life

(All of the above titles are available at your local bookstore.
Those without asterisks may be ordered by calling
Hay House at 760-431-7695 or 800-654-5126.)

Please visit the Hay House Website at: **hayhouse.com**
and Sylvia Browne's Website at: **sylvia.org**

THE NATURE
OF GOOD
AND EVIL

Sylvia Browne

HAY
HOUSE

Hay House, Inc.
Carlsbad, California • Sydney, Australia

Copyright © 2001 by Sylvia Browne

Published and distributed in the United States by:
Hay House, Inc., P.O. Box 5100, Carlsbad, CA 92018-5100 • (800) 654-5126
(800) 650-5115 (fax)

Editorial: Larry Beck, Jill Kramer • *Design:* Summer McStravick

Library of Congress Cataloging-in-Publication Data

Browne, Sylvia.
    The nature of good and evil / Sylvia Browne.
        p. cm. – (Journey of the soul series)
    The text has three voices, Sylvia and two spirit guides, Francine and
Raheim.
    ISBN 1-56170-724-4
      1. Good and evil—Miscellanea. 2. Gnosticism—Miscellanea. 3. Spiritual
life—Miscellanea. 4. Spirit writings. 5. Society of Novus Spiritus (Campbell,
Calif.) I. Francine (Spirit) II. Raheim (Spirit) III. Title.

BF1311.G63 B76 2001
133.9'3—dc21

                                            00-040-796

ISBN 1-56170-724-4

04 03 02 01   4 3 2 1
1st printing, March 2001

Printed in the United States of America

For my beloved Creators

Love is constant, unbending, unyielding,
and forever present for you.
It's the one thing created by God that's never lost.

The only pure emotions are love and happiness.
These two are sisters.

God's love is constant, outpouring, nonrestrictive,
nonjudgmental, ongoing, and forever omnipresent.

Love is the only thing that rejuvenates itself.

Love is the best thing we have to offer.
Where there is love, there can be no taint of despair,
greed, or negativity.

Partnership in love is the greatest gift God bestows.

It is in loving that you expand your soul.

— Sylvia

❦ CONTENTS ❦

This project is the result of many people working very hard to make my dream come true. This text was carefully revealed for you during many thousands of hours of research. I give my thanks to two people, Larry Beck and Mary Simonds, for their hard work and dedication to my mission in life.

§ Introduction §

THE SOCIETY OF NOVUS SPIRITUS is my church, located in Campbell, California. The tenets in this book are based on the philosophy of this church, which I founded several years ago. The knowledge contained in this book represents the integration of several sources of information. First, it reflects knowledge infused by my own psychic ability throughout many years. It also reflects my spirit guide Francine's tremendous knowledge of life's plan and of the Other Side. Additional knowledge was passed down from my psychic grandmother, Ada, who represents almost 300 years of psychic family tradition. In addition, thousands of hypnotic regressions were done independently of the other material, yet it all came together like clockwork, validating, filling in any gaps, and showing that there is a logical plan to everything God creates.

I think that we, as human beings, have lived long enough with the so-called mysteries. As Francine says, if you can think of the question, your guides will give you the answer. Indeed, my faith, Gnostic Christianity, teaches that we must always continue to seek for answers, because seeking is an essential process for spiritual growth.

I decided to make this philosophy public because of the comments I receive so often: "I've always known this. This is what I've always believed, although I couldn't put it into words. I just felt that this truth resonated in my soul as *right*." The philosophy, although extensive, comes without fear or condemnation. It comes with knowledge, but without dogma. I've always believed that everyone, no matter what their beliefs, should take with them what they need or want, and then leave the rest behind. Only occultism is hidden, secretive, and controlling; you will find none of that in these writings. Of course, certain codes for behavior are innate laws of good by which we must all live—but the part of you that's God is individual in every way.

The work in *Journey of the Soul* has three voices. Of course, my own is present, but I also have two communicating spirit guides, Francine and Raheim, who are the major contributors. Francine's voice is audible to me, but relaying her information orally isn't the most efficient form of communication. By special arrangement with God, I'm able to allow Francine and Raheim to take control of my body so that they can communicate directly with others. This is called "deep-trance mediumship," which is best known through the works of Edgar Cayce. An interesting aspect of this ability is that I retain no personal knowledge of the words or actions that occur while I'm in trance. For many years, we have done "research trances," giving us the knowledge that fills these pages. Of course, we all learn by asking questions, so you will see many such inquiries appearing in italics throughout this work. This series is truly a journey of the soul, and I'm so glad to have you along for the ride.

This material represents thousands of hours of work, so when you read it, by no means feel that you're merely reading the faint musings of a simple medium in trance. Much of the knowledge that has been garnered is extremely deep, abstract, and esoteric; you will probably prefer to read much of it in short passages instead of all at once. I hope you enjoy it, and more important, I wish that if nothing else, you come away as I have, with a magnificent obsession to learn more, explore more, and delve deeper into the great theology that's just waiting for all of us to discover.

We in the Society of Novus Spiritus find that there is great comfort in walking together in our belief, loving God without fear or guilt. To learn is spiritual, because knowledge destroys ignorance, prejudice, and greed.

God bless you. I do.

— *Sylvia*

EDITOR'S NOTE: *The following text has three voices.
Of course, Sylvia speaks, but she also has two
communicating spirit guides, Francine and Raheim,
who are the major contributors. Whenever the voice
changes on the text, it will be marked. Also, throughout
the portions authored by Francine and Raheim,
there are questions that appear in italics.*

$\S$ Chapter One $\S$

THE TRUE GOD IS LOVE

Sylvia: "I am the Lord thy God, and thou shalt not have strange gods before me," says the First Commandment brought down by Moses from Mount Sinai. Moses spent 60 days in the wilderness seeking just the right words to communicate his inspiration in terms that would impress the people of those days. But what was motivational in that ancient era of crisis needs rewording today. How could there be a jealous god? Jealousy is a human trait, not at all Divine. This passage in the Bible immediately sets the tone and tempo for a conniving, petty, jealous, malicious, vengeful god.

Moses was trying to free his people from slavery under the Egyptians. To do so, he had to make his god more powerful, mean, vengeful, and jealous. But the problem is, we never let go of this interpretation. Even today, we are told to "fear God," but I cannot.

Sadly, the First Commandment creates fear, which is the antithesis of love.

In fact, fear is a powerful force that thrives on this planet, having found its home here. It is nourished, it flourishes, and it's alive and well, usually existing in all of us. But the adage, "There is nothing to fear but fear itself," is very true.

The Gnostics, who go back to the beginning of time, knew a

force with no real interest in us.

What about the lost days and minutes that pass in this futile activity? Do you know that if you live to be 80 years old, you will have lived about 700,000 hours? That isn't a lot. Try to have $700,000 in the bank. It's absolutely finite. And anyone may go at any given time. This is why we must cherish life, and know the true God.

Sometimes when you give it all up—give up all those false gods—you get the real one.

Man-Made Rituals

Going back over a lot of the books that profess the Mother God, we see that, tragically, those who revere Her have always been labeled a cult. Sadly, a belief in Mother God has always carried a stigma. Two books, *Holy Blood, Holy Grail* and *Messianic Legacy,* speak of this very strongly. Yet we know that a loving, maternal consciousness is breaking upon us, which is as old as time. That's why I really regret the perception of ours as a "New Age" religion. We're not. As a resurgence of Gnosticism, we are an "Old Age" religion. This is a time of renewal in which all of the old and wonderful things come back, renewed, without the baggage of repressed cultures and judgment.

Take the principle, "Honor thy father and thy mother." It seems to be so clear, so succinct, doesn't it? What you don't know is that it really referred to Mother and Father God! Honor the Mother God, who is the Mother of Creation, and the Father God, the source of knowledge.

I said to Francine, my spirit guide, "What if you really don't feel like you want to honor your parents?" She said, "You need only honor them if they're *honorable*." That cleared it up for me.

Also, today you don't really have to give people respect if they're not respectable. What if someone is mean, hateful, and nasty to you? Say you walk in the room where your children are watching TV, you change the channel they're watching, and you don't say *please* or *I'm sorry*. Do you think that those kids are going to have much respect for you? You have been disrespectful to them.

We can't wait for our children to talk, can we? Some of us regret they ever learned how by the time they become teenagers. "Oh, isn't that cute, how my little baby is babbling," we say when they can't be understood. Then eventually they really talk and talk. At that point, we still expect this formerly little person to be quiet whenever it suits us.

When I was teaching school, I would refer to my students as "little people," because that's what they are. Little people with souls. Little people with feelings and fully intact memories, who can only honor their parents if they're honorable and respectable.

Now, what if we take it further? It's widely accepted by historians that Gnosticism goes back as far as any recorded knowledge texts, very often under the term *nature religion*. Churches have tried to suppress it, but unsuccessfully. That came out in the Nag Hammadi (the location in Egypt where many ancient scrolls were uncovered, similar to the Dead Sea Scrolls); it became obvious in many sources. People are finding new knowledge in the Dead Sea Scrolls, the suppressed written words, and many books that were deleted from the Bible. Tragically, some scrolls haven't been found yet, including parts of James, Timothy, and Thomas.

The ancient belief says that even Moses was part of the Gnostic movement.[2] It encompassed many of the Jews and other thinking people of that time, but they always had to go underground because of political opposition. Gnostics were usually considered heretics because they questioned the authority and wisdom of the hierarchy.

Be *reasonable*. That's all we ask you to do. Think in your own logical mind, using both intellect and emotion, male and female, working together. You're both. You have a male side of your brain, known as intellect; and an emotional side, known as feminine. You couldn't have been made from only one side of a Creator, the unmoving Father's mind. If that's the case, where do we women come from? If we are a genetic stamp from a rib of Adam, please help me! No, even Genesis says, "We created man . . ."—go read it for yourself.

I went through theology classes hoping that I could find some truth in them. I kept arguing and fighting with the instructors. They didn't know what to do with me. They figured I had somewhat of a brain, plus I was a Jewish girl and a Christian convert, so they didn't want to kick me out. But I was troublesome.

Gnostics always address and challenge the issues of the day. If there is any one book in the Bible that's Gnostic, it's Leviticus, which gives rules of hygiene and of right action. It's not dogmatic, however.

Please realize that much of the Old Testament is instructive, but not Divine, discourse. The reason why Jews were forbidden to eat pork in those days was actually because pork was dirty, and there were no curative methods available at that time. So when people became ill as a result of eating poorly cooked pork, the Jews said, "We're not going to risk our people eating this." This was a man-made decision, not an edict from God.

Do you realize that during the time of the plague, the Jews were mostly untouched by the disease? Many others thought that they were all witches and warlocks because they were the only ones who believed in bathing. And their food preparation rules ensured good health. Others were eating animals that were already long dead and disease-ridden.

So the Jewish people were healthy and clean, while most of Western Europe didn't believe in bathing. You know how you see everyone in movies wearing those gorgeous, medieval gowns? In truth, they were far from spotless, because their owners rarely bathed, nor washed their clothes; they didn't believe in it.

These old laws that have become dogma are exactly why we must use our own, God-given powers of reason. What kind of insanity do we impose on God? What kind of a maniac have we envisioned in a god that plays "Russian roulette" with people's lives? A god that hates one person and sends him a lot of unbearable pain, and then is really good to another person? What kind of a god is that?

It was not too surprising when eventually people started saying, "God is dead."

No wonder they did. The god that they envisioned either died or never was. The Gnostics say, "No, God is omnipotent, a perfect unit. Complete and gorgeous, magnified billions of times, with unconditional *love*." Unconditional love is funny: A parent may rant and rave about their children or not like them at all, but can you show me any parent who wouldn't give up their life for their children? And we're human. Now take that concept, but magnify it to God's level. Why then do people think that God is going to "damn" them? We give our souls away, not relying upon ourselves. Gnosticism can tell you truths—but you yourself must envision and act upon your own truth, live your own truth.

We come together because that gives us more power as we grow spiritually. Form a body of people who are united in thought and belief, because it makes a more powerful arrow to pierce the darkness of ignorance.

Gnostics are piercing—we ask everyone to think.

God is all-loving and caring. Allow this truth to generate for you the God that we love, honor, and serve.

People always ask if I tell the truth to my clients. A man wrote to me: "You were the only one who told me that my son was going to die." I had said, "You will have him 16 months. He will come and go, and then his life force will depart." This was a horrible message to deliver, but I did so.

He said, "It turned out to be 16 and a half months. But I heard from some people that God took him from me." That would be a god who plays Russian roulette again, wouldn't it? Any god who says, "I want your child" is so cruel. How can God be unfeeling and uncaring?

The loving God, the caring God, the omnipotent God, doesn't create pain. Some people claim they're "better" than others, and God "loves" them more. That's *never* true. Isn't God everything?

Nobody realizes that all the great, ancient prophets had the same basic message. What happens after the prophet comes, whether it's Buddha or Mohammed? The simple truth begins to be "explained" by the disciples through interpretation and rebuttal to existing beliefs.

It leads to a man-made perversion of the original message. I hope that after I'm gone, my beliefs stay pure, keeping the Mother God concept and the emphasis on forgiveness and common sense.

Within our loving, are we allowed to have righteous anger and fight back? You bet. Because to be anything else is wimpy. Most of what we fight in life is simple ignorance. Sit and listen to people discuss their beliefs, and note how sincerely they're attached to them for their own "salvation." You realize that there is *no* thinking going on, that only fear and tradition hold power. But, as I've said thousands of times, thinking will never be for everyone.

Many people don't want to think. They want to turn over their soul to somebody else to "save" it. That's why people send in their money to televangelists. I'm not judging these people, but they themselves will tell you, "If I send in $20, then my soul is saved." And that's sad.

You, along with God, are the salvation of your own soul. You never need an intermediary.

You were saved when you came into life. God wouldn't have put you here unattended. You live within the influence of the Mother God, too. The Catholic church was smart about this when they exchanged Mary for "Mother God." Most religions have a primary female entity, such as the Lady of the Lotus in Buddhism. Even Jesus was trying to bring in the female entity; whether Mary Magdalene, his own mother, or simply women in general. We've forgotten that feminine side of ourselves. We see what happens with pure, unbalanced patriarchy: namely, Inquisitions, Holy Wars, Crusades, and so on. Some think if you bring in the maternal side of Creation, then the whole masculine side is diminished. No. It's enhanced—the wondrous completeness of our Duality. Our Lord said this, didn't he?

He said, "What God has joined together, let no man put asunder."

We've split the intellect and the emotion, not only away from ourselves, but in our religious beliefs. We've taken away the emotional side. Intellect by itself becomes oppressive and devoid of humanity. Then we get fanatics, don't we? Is there anything worse? I don't care whether it occurs in business, with parents, with a spouse, whatever it might be.

Fanaticism is insanity. When you're in a rational, reasoning state, you can't get fanatical.

That's why you will never find fanaticism in Gnostic Christianity, because we balance intellect and emotion. We self-audit and adjust. It's not easy. Like I said, our philosophy can be stated in about one paragraph, but to live it is very difficult.

You have to think. You have to search. You have to read. You have to be constantly wary of ignorance. When we come into human form, we immediately get stupid. One problem is that we're constantly barraged by our physical needs: We're too hot or cold; our bones feel too heavy or too fragile; we have to eat and excrete; we have to work despite our headaches in order to survive and feed our kids. Just surviving is tough!

Then we are told to add religion on top of that, not realizing that survival *is* religious and spiritual. Because we're doing it for God.

Living, breathing, doing, and caring for people is a prayer by example. People ask, "Do you pray?" I say, "Every day of my life is a prayer; I take care of people." I would much rather be helping six people than be kneeling silently for three hours. How beneficial is that?

People say, "I pray all the time." Great, but then go do something for others, too. Go to convalescent hospitals, help the poor, talk to people; be loving, caring, considerate, and watchful. We as a group want to take care of each other. We want to bring people into our caring. We want to take care of the aged and children, to create a society that celebrates the family group. If one of us doesn't have enough food, I want to give them food. That's what Gnosticism is about. We go and fetch and carry and help.

To serve God is to serve Their people. The only way we're going to make it economically anymore, is in community living. Other cultures have known this. We've been stupid. We got away from it. We have to live as a community. We have to live as mutually caring people.

Say, "I'm there for you." Then God's presence is among us. God is here. God is with us. Rather than saying, "Did you see so-and-so and what she was wearing? I think she looks like hell."

That's all part of the human experience. But if someone in our church were hurt, you better believe everybody is there. That's what it means to have a family community group.

You know the group that really makes this work is the Amish community. They do. Not that I want all of us to go buy a farm and till the fields and all that. But look at that way of life as something beautiful. Severe as it may be, it is beautiful.

There are too many people walking around with a heavy heart, thinking, *I'm not going to be saved.* Saved from what? The only thing you have to be saved from is yourself, what you absorb, and how much pain you internalize. There is no other salvation beyond that.

Don't you know that God wants you to be happy? Why make such an awful god? You say, "Oh, God really hates me." What? He has nothing to do except look at your name, and say, "I hate him or her"?

Stupid. That makes God too human. God isn't human, and what difference does it make what we call God? Whether we call Him *Yahweh, Allah,* or *Sophia.* That doesn't matter to God.

God is all-loving and always there for us. The word *forgiveness* is about *giving.* Chop the word in two—*for-giving.*

For giving, to me, is what I want to be. I love to be forgiving to you, but I have to first forgive myself. I have to give to me, and love me. Every great thinker said, "Love your neighbor as yourself." We said, "Yes, I can love my neighbors, and *sometimes* me, but then I feel too selfish."

Wrong. You're a part of God. The finger of God moves through you just as strongly as it does the Pope, any bishop, or me. The fact that you do not give sermons doesn't mean you're not as advanced. You may be more so. Someone who ends up in the spotlight may just be the infusing channel at that time, but then they go away, and another takes their place.

Racial Prejudice

Oh, please believe me, there are evil entities with every shade of skin. You know you have met them. "Oh," you say, "I think everybody is good." Haven't you known some people who you just have to get away from? They will pollute you—but even they are here for a purpose. You can say in all righteousness, "There but for the grace of God go I."

There is a dark type of entity that doesn't ever want to go to the Other Side and wants to keep reincarnating. They just keep coming back and coming back. This is their planet. When you come up against one of these dark entities, you will know it. Every alarm goes off; you feel drained; you get that sinking feeling in your stomach.

Raheim: Racial prejudice is the handmaiden of soul-dark entities. Until we form a brotherhood, loving each other for who we are, there will never be peace in the world. We must cross those racial barriers and fight against the darkness that preaches, "We must keep our race pure; we must keep our species pure."

The heart knows who it wants to love. If someone wants to marry outside their race, that's nothing of consequence in the mind and heart of God. There shouldn't even be a word such as *interracial.*

When Mother Azna appears to Hispanics, She is Hispanic. She is called Mary by the Catholics. When She appears to African Americans, She appears black. Does that give you any indication that She has no color differentiation? When She appeared as "The Lady of Guadalupe," She didn't come with blonde hair and blue eyes.

Once you begin to differentiate between the races or the creeds, you have now made God just white. Do you think that the Jesus that hung on a cross was only a white man? No. He encompassed every group. If that wasn't the case, then God would have made only one species, and only either male or female. If it was the case that you were supposed to stay with only your own "kind," you should just stay with females or males. Now, of course, society has created another prejudice against gays, which is another crucifixion pattern.

What your message should be is that you accept all races into your heart—and you can't say, "I believe that other races are good, but I don't want my family to have anything to do with them." That's prejudicial. You're now putting conditions on love.

When the world understands this, then the brutality stops. The prejudice has got to stop. You have got to live by the teachings of the spiritual masters such as Jesus and the Buddha.

We've got to stop persecuting each other. What is so ironic is that everyone has been every race and creed in past lifetimes. Do you think that because you're now a certain race, you haven't been black or yellow or red before? Of course you have. Maybe you were not treated right then, but that was for your perfection scheme.

Francine: Please notice that most of what you think of as "primitive" cultures were the most advanced spiritually—the Aztecs, Native Americans, Africans, and certain aspects of the Viking and early Celtic cultures. I'm saying this solely because it's absolutely true. Primitive is simplistic, close to God, shamanistic. Aborigines, of course, have kept their culture—their dream-times, medicine men, and magic. They still know how to walk with God.

We find that only in your culture—primarily on the North American continent—does this kind of strangeness occur, where people have such a division of color. We've never been able to understand that at all. It is ridiculous.

You will find that the more spiritual you become, the more primitive your soul becomes again. It loses those outer layers of the superficial culture, and goes back to the earth, the ground, the leaves, the grass, the herbs, the holistic. You know for a fact that everything in modern medicine is taken from some herb. Everything— I don't care what they call it—is derived from something in nature that they have copied.

Some are saying that in America in your time, the races are being absorbed. I don't see that. I think that the Hispanics, the Native

Americans, the African Americans, and the Asians are stronger and have kept their culture. Contrast this with the Sumerians—how many of them do you see around? There are none. How many Aztecs or Mayans do you see? They have been absorbed. The culture that I lived in has been almost totally disintegrated, which is tragic.

Raheim: The darkness takes prejudice, greed, and drug addictions and works those weaknesses for its own advantage. There are such things as dark entities that roam this planet—we all know that from the previous books of this series. They can only attack you in an unwary moment, but you don't have to stand for the attack. Because your actual essence, which is God, can't be attacked or hurt in any way.

When you start thinking of yourself as a flame of light, then so much of the world's negativity doesn't affect you. I'm trying to help you see that you're impervious to wrongdoings against you. Many of the slings and arrows that you're hit by are verbal abuses. Maybe we should think about having discipline of the mouth, because words fly too quickly at times. Now, it isn't so much your fault. It's the irritation and stress of the world.

Many times people are not given to the art of communication. That's no one's fault. No one is taught. On my side, because we're very psychically and telepathically knowledgeable, we understand the heart, no matter what comes out of the mouth. You're denied this privilege, and that's part of the test.

How many times have you had something hurtful said to you, then walked right back into that circle to get it again? There is something almost masochistic about being human—not only do you want to be bludgeoned once, but you walk back for more. What you're doing is giving the other person power. Nothing deflects darkness better in your business and personal life than to walk away. Otherwise, the person on the attack can keep coming.

However, I'm sure a lot of you are often surprised at what comes out of your mouth. You have put the other person on the defensive unnecessarily. If you heard someone say the very same thing to you, how would it feel? This isn't to make you become meek. In Gnosticism, there is nothing meek. The Gnostics have always been fighters, warriors, crusaders. They always want to jump onto a horse and go riding off. They're the first to rush off for a cause.

Gnosis—A Way of Living

Sylvia: People ask, "What do you mean by Gnostic Christianity?"

Actually we were not Gnostic *Christians* until the second word was coined, which was, of course, after the time of Jesus. Before that, we were just Gnostics and Essenes. This was a group of people that Jesus belonged to. We simply believe in reincarnation, in an all-loving and fair God, and in the Mother God principle. We studied where we were going and why we were here. We charted our life—bad and good—as the experiencing part of God, and we sent this information back to the Divine source.

Most other churches built big buildings and begged everybody for money. The Gnostics wanted to be, and still are, a group of people that have a hand in the community to help, pray for people, have meditation groups, and go about loving and experiencing for God without the pomp and ceremony. Regardless of what you have ever been, you can also be one of us, a Gnostic.

A Gnostic doesn't believe something without proof, without basis. We must research and validate. But many people are lazy. They won't go out and read the history of their own religion, much less how religions began. Do not just believe what I say—you should go out and look up the Nag Hammadi, the writings of the Essenes, and see if the words are not written down exactly. The writers of these words were not beginning Bible students. No. They believed and thought of the Bible as a metaphor that teaches the greatness of God. The Gnostic writings were stymied by the "Pauline" Christians because the Gnostics didn't encourage fear and control.

People go to church, they thought, *because they're afraid of going to hell.* Well, too bad, they're already there. This is it. So you don't have much to be afraid of anymore. You are in the worst place you will ever be in. It's *here*. Instead of being afraid of demons and devils, what we realize as Gnostics is that we have to fight *our own* negativity. In doing that, we're celebrating our own God-centeredness. We understand that material things are fleeting, but spiritual values are forever.

We also must understand that every age is afraid of the so-called Antichrist. My dear friends, since the time Christ died, you have been in the age of the Antichrist. That term only means being against everything that Jesus wanted us to know: the loving, beautiful, forgiving, omnipotent, constant God. Not the God who brings about fear and horror and hate and Holy Wars.

So we're the White Brotherhood, meaning that we're the group that dedicates themselves to carrying God's light and becoming the avatars of the world. *Avatars* are the teachers and mission life entities.

It's amazing to me that, one way or another, most Gnostics will find each other. The only other group that I know of is in Brazil. They have been fighting their way through to get in touch with us. I had one emissary that came to visit me. They have already heard about us.

So there is some kind of telepathic drum that beats at night, saying, "There is another group." They will spring up all over. When truth comes out, it comes out all over. Now, others call us the "New Age." If anything, every religion you know of is the "New Age"— Lutheran, Episcopalian, Baptist, Presbyterian.

We are even older than what they call the "Wiccans." There was no religion before us. Gnosticism was the religion of the world at one time, when the world was interested in knowledge. If the libraries of Alexandria hadn't burned, you would have seen it. Which makes you really wonder who burned it, doesn't it? Yet no one can stifle the truth forever.

The White Brotherhood means the groups of people—the Gnostics, the Essenes—who have come back into life to gather together and make this world right, because of the evil that abounds.

Don't ever think there isn't. We, as Gnostics, believe that there is evil. But we believe that it's created by the human soul. It can become so strong that it can actually form something very bad.

God did not make a devil. He couldn't have. Think of it logically. How can something *all good, all loving, perfect, intrinsically and omnipotently good* make something bad? If He did, He had to have something bad, and He didn't. He cannot, will not, and never did. God in His Creation is ongoing. He is a noninterfering God who allows us to evolve as we will according to our charts, which are contracts between us and God.

There was a study in which people with cancer were divided into two groups. Half were prayed over, and half were not. The group having prayer improved, and the other didn't. Why does this work, if our chart defines our life? Because of the energy. You can still have cancer, but just a little one that can be taken out. You can program that.

Everything can be the way it's supposed to be in the chart, but soften it with your prayers.

Rationality and Awareness

The Age of Aquarius—what does that mean? I think what Francine, my spirit guide, was saying to me the other night makes so much sense. I'm always thrown off by the simplicity of her words in place of the complexity that I create. It was right in front of my eyes. Francine said, "This isn't the Age of Aquarius. It's the Age of Internal Awareness." People are starting to open up their minds, and are no longer held by old dogma such as fear and guilt.

The Age of Awareness—more truly, of Rationality—is dawning.

This religion will never be for everyone. Most people still want to have their minds ruled, their lives ruled, and what's more horrendous, their souls ruled. It's a tragedy. With this Age of Awareness, we can only offer an alternative to blind faith. We do not advocate converting others; rather, when they are ready, then they will find us.

We intellectually seek God through reason, as Jesus did. The tragedy is that the more aware you become, the more you realize how close-minded most people are. It's a double-edged sword, isn't it? For as aware as you are, what great heights can you reach? If you're walking around numb and are not aware, you will have to do it at some point somewhere. That isn't my say-so. That's logic.

Have you ever tried to ignore a well-established pattern in your life without working through it? "Well, I don't choose to deal with that now," you said, and what happened? You had to deal with it eventually. It might have come in a different form—a different face or circumstance—but you had to face it. So we never really skip it.

Knowledgeably and rationally, as followers of truth, we can choose not to go through certain situations. But keep in mind that we will have to face that pattern again. No one escapes it. The only difference is that when we do face it, we will know what we're facing.

Many people say, "I don't know what it's all about; I don't know what God is thinking; I don't know where I am; I don't know what I believe."

But, Gnostics do know. There may be many variables in your life you don't like, but always know that you picked each one of them. You chose them. You're living through each for a reason. You may not like it, but at some level you know what the point is.

We're away from Home right now at "Boot Camp." We're going to learn a lot of skills. Once we get those, we're going back Home and stay there. It's sort of like college, but I like to call it "Boot Camp." We have to just tough it out, and eventually we graduate.

In between, why come to church? Being together creates a feeling of grace, a feeling of hope. The only way you're going to reach God is through each other.

Earth is the alien area. Rather than look to heaven and scream at the Omnipotent God who holds us tightly in His hand, anyway, relate to the god within yourself and each other. That's what God intended us to do. That's the whole allegory of Adam and Eve being tossed out of the Garden of Eden. You're supposed to go down, that is, leave heaven, and experience. Why were they tossed out? For gaining knowledge. Do you see how that all fits together?

Why do you suppose that the "knowledge of good and evil" is not available in heaven? Because in a perfect environment, there is no adversity. The snake, which represented Earth and physical life, was supposed to be the "tempter." Now how they went from "snake" to "Satan" in a red outfit is beyond me. Nothing I've ever read makes the connection. The few uses of "Satan" in the New Testament simply translate (from Aramaic) into "adversary" or "wrong thinking." In fact, on Gethsemane, Jesus actually says, "Get thee behind me, Satan." He was not speaking to the soldiers; rather, he said it to the apostle Peter. So you can either believe that "Satan" is Peter, or simply that Jesus told Peter he was wrong and to step back.

Stop with the devil. Quit giving him so much energy. Now, are there evil entities that roam the earth? Yes, they walk among us in suits and dresses, and they drive cars. They're not devils. They're mean *people*. Even they have their place. If we were all sweetness and light, with no differences in personality, what would be the challenge? What would be the stimulation for us to test our soul?

On the Other Side, we all keep our own personalities. Now, that doesn't make me too happy, knowing some personalities as I do. But the nice thing about it is, we don't have to associate with those people if we don't want to. Let's say that a person has the life theme of Irritant. (A list of all 45 life themes can be found in Book 2 of the *Journey of the Soul* series: *Soul's Perfection*.) Those people come down so we can learn what? Tolerance. Patience. Did you ever notice how Irritants do their job so well?

What is the purpose of coming to church? The very act of finding a true church, a true belief, a true philosophy begins to open up your channels and infuse you with knowledge and grace. If you don't open these channels, you wander around with no connection to the Divine. Humans were supposed to socially meet, talk to, and be with others and receive grace.

Communion is doing something collectively. Our Lord said, "Do this in remembrance of me." The giving of food and the taking-in is a social amenity. It's a charitable, social, healing amenity. It's like the chicken-soup remedy: "You're sick, so let me give you lots of water and soup to drink." A person gets well sooner with chicken soup, not because of the soup, but due to the love that goes into the soup.

Always keep in front of you the focus of why you're here. I must do that daily for myself. I say, "Wait a minute. What is it all for?" In my case, I want Novus to grow worldwide so people stop with the fear and the guilt and the hellfire that stunts spiritual growth.

You can't accelerate, you can't channel, you can't hear God speak, you can't have your own burning bush if you're stymied by fear and guilt. You must stop, because fear is the true "Antichrist." Do you want to know where the Antichrist is? It's among us.

Don't let anyone take over your soul. Don't let anyone tell you how you should live. Be aware. Be outward functioning, caring. Reach your hands out to other people. That's what my church is about. Grace is coming together and touching each other's God-center. That's what it's about. I promise you, your life will get better through every adversity.

Once you find the truth, once you find the golden pot at the end of the rainbow, a wonderful dome seems to come down over you and says, "I'm here for you. You finally reached Me. You reached up through your own mind, through your own center, and you found Me."

So God *has been* there, and so God *is* there, and so God *will always be.* He is found through reason and Light. That's what the avatars were trying to tell everybody, and what happened to them? They were swept aside, and many died at the hands of those who couldn't hear the message.

Then the avatars were made into gods—which was the last thing they wanted. In the Sermon on the Mount, Jesus said, "Listen to me. Pray this way: 'Our Father, who art in Heaven, hallowed be thy name.'" He never said, "Pray to me." He said, "Pray this way."

We have lost our loving God, and we complicated the teachings of every messiah. Now we're going back to what the masters wanted, to what they believed in, and the way they lived their lives. I saw a minister on television. He had The Book in his hand and was screaming, "But that isn't what the scripture really means. What Jesus said was this, however, what he *really* meant was . . ."

I thought, *How dare you. How ostentatious of you.* How would you like to think that in years to come someone took your words, and said, "Oh, but that isn't what he meant. *I'm* going to tell you what he meant." It's horrifying that this happens. Jesus' words are clear, and so were those of all the other prophets that came.

But everyone thinks their ego is so big that they can interpret it, "*I* will tell you what he *meant*. He meant you're going to go to hell." They always have that hook in there, "You're going to hell. You're going to be punished."

But you know what happens is that they drone at you until one day you say, "Wait a minute. Something is wrong. I want to believe in an all-loving, nonvengeful, nonjealous God."

They make God human, don't they? In doing that, they lose God.

It's like the First Commandment: "I am the Lord thy God, and thou shalt not have strange gods before me." What kind of a god says that? Who does he have to be jealous of? The Egyptian gods? The Persian gods? It's all the same God. What difference does it make what name is used?

Stop with the prejudice and the judgment and the self-righteousness.

Aren't we all moving toward one God? We're so fragile, aren't we? "My name is Sylvia. Please don't take that away from me, because I won't be identified. Please don't take my car away, either. You will only know me because of the car I drive. Please don't take my house, because it's the place I live and you know my address. Please don't take my telephone number."

Just be yourself. Be the best "you" that you know how to be.

Let us have the purpose:
to give other people hope,
to keep our family units together,
to keep the whole moral fiber of ourselves intact,
to give love and sanction and grace to everyone we meet.
We are "Grace Givers."
　　　　— Sylvia

---

[1] See Book 2 in the *Journey of the Soul* series, *Soul's Perfection*, for a complete discussion of charting your life.

[2] We believe that Moses was the Pharaoh Amenhotep IV (who renamed himself Akhenaton), who attempted to bring monotheism to Egypt.

Sylvia calls it the passive mind, and that's right, except that the passive and the power source are all the same. So is the super-conscious—they are all the same mind. Within each mind there is emotion and intellect.

Now you say, "Do you mean to tell me I am three people dupli-cated?" In a way, you are. The etheric mind has an emotional side that can be fearful from past-life situations. It also has the ability to be euphoric and blissful—although that doesn't stay very long, does it? So once in a while you do get the euphoria and bliss, but you can't keep it for very long. You couldn't hold it. This is the descent of your own God-self, connected with the true God-self, that has become cemented together.

The more you reach up to the etheric mind, the more you become detached from the world. You should aspire to this. Now you may think that I say this because I come from a culture that puts aside worldly things. No, I don't. I've never described to you, only in synoptic pieces, of what my life was like in A.D. 800. I was a teacher. Like Siddhartha, I also came from a very wealthy fam-ily. I didn't want. Why that was important is I was able to travel and teach, and not have to worry about whether I had bread on my plate or not. So I was very fortunate. In that time, most of us, like you eventually will be, were traveling teachers. Teaching wasn't held so much in temples or in groups like Jesus had. Jesus was fol-lowing the same type of church or temple tradition of what we call "the caravan teachers." Those were the ones that went out on the road, not unlike the later evangelists. Except Jesus didn't have ben-efit of tents, and I did.

The point is, I began to be more and more removed, and put myself upon the charity of others. Only because I didn't care for the things of the world. Did I enjoy a good meal? Yes. Did I enjoy laughter and a nice glass of wine? Yes. But I found that as I became older—and I lived to be quite elderly—I began to be more removed.

I found that the "magnificent obsession," as Sylvia calls it, became all-encompassing. The peacefulness and the bliss become the most blessed of addictions. To remove yourself and know that all these things pass, and to be in service for God, is truly the etheric mind.

Now, the amazing benefit to that is the more possessions you begin to give up, the more they don't mean that much to you. I don't mean give up your houses or your nice things or your cars or your children. That's ridiculous. The strange thing about the phenomenon of grace is that it comes more when there is less clutter.

The root of all evil isn't gold. It's *love* of gold, or greed, that creates evil.

Loving anything on the worldly plane too much can create a backlash effect. Now, I'm not by any means telling you that loving people has a backlash. That's encompassing the God-center to make it more full.

How do you reach this etheric mind? It's always reached, strangely enough, in a very light, meditative state. It's not in a deep sleeping state. It's ridiculous to think that you need to be unconscious to reach it. All you need to do is lie down and breathe. In fact, before this session is over, I will show you a way to get to there.

Now, let us discuss what we call the middle mind. This is the processing mind, the perfunctory mind, the work mind. It has creative force, but not unless the channel is open to the etheric mind. It's what I call the "you mind." The middle mind is where you're living in the world, what you're doing, what you seem to identify yourself with, and what you're operating on. It seems to be the sum total of your personality in this life. So it's basically your uniqueness.

Is the etheric mind as unique? No. When it's reached, the etheric mind becomes more universal, although it remains your own private mind. You're tapping in to what Buddhists and many others thought was a nirvana state. The middle mind is the essence of you as yourself in life and on the Other Side; it's your persona, that which keeps you individually carved. It's your quirks and your smirks, your personality and your sensitivities, your sensibilities and all the other things that make you up individually.

Now we get to the nemesis, the lower mind. This is the basic, instinctual mind that preserves the self. We refer to it as the "caveman mind." The problem with the instinctual mind is that it leaks up. When the etheric mind leaks down, that's wonderful. I don't want you to put a cap on that. But you get into problems when the lower mind begins to leak up.

"I want liquor or chocolate all the time; it tastes good. I want to do this. I want to serve myself—to reward myself—in any way I can." It's the vehicle-destroying part of the mind. It wasn't that way in early times, because there was nothing really available unless you wanted to smoke hemp. So when you're throttled by addictions, this is different from the paranoid state that can come from past lives leaking down. When you become addicted to things of the flesh, that's the lower mind leaking upward.

You can cap that off by saying, "I want my lower, base self— my instinctual, animal, survival side—to stay in its rightful place." Keep the "I Am" intact. Let the leak come from the top down, but allow no leak from the bottom up. Otherwise you become like a child who wants and grabs and needs and cries and is petulant.

Each of these three selves is definitive, yet they all belong to you. Notice how this trinity replicates that between the Father, Mother, and Holy Spirit, which is nothing more than the love between Father and Mother God, and between every human being— between our Gods, us, and each other. The upper mind is the Mother: nurturing, giving, remembering, guiding. The middle mind is the Father: static, continuous, all-purpose, all-knowing. That doesn't make Him lower. The lower self is only of this world.

On the Other Side, you only have the middle and upper self. You don't have the lower self. That's the detriment to most of humankind. There is no control. You're now seeing a widespread phenomenon going on in your world where the lower self rules. The aesthetic self no longer rules, except in your Gnostic belief.

The lower self says, "Bear arms, have gangs, and go shoot people." That's worse than caveman tactics, because even primitive people only fought for their rights or their territory. There is no longer any conditioned reflex of anything coming from the higher mind or the "I Am."

We find that the lower mind dominates very much in what's called "the public arena." People cheer when others are torn to shreds by lions. People stop and stare at accidents and crime scenes.

It's the same thing when your society wanted to televise an execution, because they thought it would be the highest-rated program. That's something very sickening and brutal. Remember when TV constantly played the Rodney King beating? As horrifying as that was, we saw everyone continue to watch it repeatedly. Not that it didn't need to be seen, but the gruesomeness of replaying the beating over and over was horrifying.

Human beings do the same thing with the crucifixion of Jesus. They keep reenacting it and reenacting it. There is something grossly horrifying about watching a beloved prophet, a beloved minister from God, constantly going through the agonies of the damned. How does it benefit us to see the vileness of life, or the horrors that other people can perpetrate upon another person?

People who do this, though, always say so sweetly, "It's so we don't forget." How many times does a hideous thing like that have to be imprinted upon your mind for you to always remember?

We see the darkness in the soul. You will eventually see it, too. If you were drawn to read this, then you're certainly spiritual enough to get the signal immediately.

How does despair operate?

It pulls you into the lower mind. Within despair is futility, and in futility, you truly become earthbound. And becoming earthbound, you get into the "poor me" syndrome. Then you really begin to reside *in* the body instead of *above* the body.

Are earthbound spirits dark?

Take, for instance, the one that has been the most publicized—Johnny Johnson, the "ghost" at Toys-R-Us (in Sunnyvale, California), who was investigated by Sylvia. He has an obsessive love for Beth, who has been dead for more than 100 years now. He is stubborn, selfish, and not about to leave. He is convinced she is going to come back and be with him, and he creates his own reality. He isn't an evil entity, but you might call him "stupid."

Most stubbornness is definitely a part of stupidity. It's not smart to be stubborn. People say, "I will be *right* to my death." Not against logic you won't, because you will come back and do it again. Regardless of whether you're on your last life or not, if you go off track and become stubbornly wrong, trust me, before Father and Mother God, you will come back and do it again, because that's part of ego. I can't think of a worse fate.

Be very careful when you're stubbornly right; make sure you *are* right.

Take, for instance, Mary Ellen Morley, a ghost who is convinced that she wants to stay on Earth simply to outlast Anna Philbrick, another ghost in the same location. These two are earthbound at Moss Beach Distillery. They are both waiting for a certain man to choose one of them. It's petty, ridiculous, and earthbinding. Do I subscribe to having partners? Of course, partnership in love is the greatest gift God bestows. You came in with the need for partnership. But if you make partnership the ultimate goal, without being a partner to yourself, you have then moved into the lower self.

Partners come in many shapes and forms, don't they? They come as children, as friends, as pets, and as a group like you coming together in fellowship. I'm constantly amazed to hear so many of you saying how lonely you are, even when you're in a group of people who love each other.

The only reason you're lonely is that you haven't *given out* love.

Your guides help you open the higher levels. They constantly try to nudge you not only through life, but into the higher realms. In fact, that's why I'm speaking to you about all this information. The ancients would sit on mountaintops for 30 years to figure out that they had to get to the higher self in their own mind.

It's all within your own self. Ask to be there. It's as simple as that. But the Guide is constantly trying to infuse you through that channel, because that's where the Guides can enter.

Is the pituitary gland our connection with the etheric mind?

Yes, it's a physical connection, as the ancient Asians knew. That's why they put a stone or a precious object right in the middle of the forehead, because it was the "all-seeing eye." If a brain scan was done on Sylvia, which she has always wanted to have done, it would show that she has highly developed pituitary and pineal glands. It's genetic through her family.

Now, did she choose to have this be so? Yes, but everyone nurtured it—the same as Angelia, Sylvia's granddaughter, is nurtured. Sylvia has always said that if her grandmother hadn't nurtured her, possibly she wouldn't have been a psychic. Yes, she would have.

To nurture your own psychic ability, you must start by clearing away the mental garbage. It can be the most beautiful edifice in the world, but if it has garbage in the front, a lot of people don't want to enter. Your job is to get rid of that mess.

Some are fearful of their garbage and even a few sleeping dragons. But once you face your dragons, you may find it's nothing more than yourself in a costume. Face it and take a leap of faith. The Gnostics were great at leaps of faith, whether it was leaping into lions' dens or wherever else they leaped. They leaped into places where no one would go because they wanted to advance faster.

Is there any danger being in the etheric mind too much?

No, there isn't, although they used to think that going out of your body too much was dangerous. You won't neglect your body. The only danger is if you're out too much, then you might need to elongate your life in order to fulfill your chart.

Since you would like to know how to reach the etheric mind, let us do a meditation to get to it. It's very simple, very easy. I would like for you to do it in a trinity number. If you're going to do it once today, try to do it two other times.

I will warn you about this, though: If you're going to do this now, I'm going to put a codicil at the end that you're going to sleep. Because you won't go to sleep tonight if you don't put the codicil on the end that you're going to go to sleep.

Because in clearing out the garbage, you're going to be in this euphoria, and you're going to be up all night. There is nothing bad about being up all night, though. People worry about that; I can't imagine why. Because you will be tired the next day? No. If you program yourself to be tired the next day, you will, but not otherwise. No one ever died from lack of sleep. People are more apt to die from too much sleep.

MEDITATION—REACHING THE ETHERIC MIND

Put your hands upward on your thighs. Close your eyes very slowly. Visualize an ancient, cobblestoned road, whose cracks are filled with beautiful green moss. Something about this road seems very familiar to you. It winds very slightly to the right and then to the left. You're amazed that you're on an incline, and yet there is no breathlessness. You're almost gliding along.

As you move to the right, it spirals upward into the mists of the clouds and mountaintops; you can look over the side and see all the beautiful greenery. Then you move to the left and look over. You're not bothered by the great drop in height, because your eyes are so riveted to where you're approaching. All of a sudden, out of the fog and the mist, a gigantic edifice comes: golden-bronze, gabled, and arched. Your eyes are struck by the sunlight that shines upon it.

Then your eyes move down the portal to the very opening of the door. You're faced with debris. The debris can come in the form of a hologram—in different postures, you may see a dancing girl, a male warrior, a Samurai, a farmer, a gypsy maiden, or a nun. They may appear agonized, leprous, ill, charming, or maybe beguiling. You see bits and pieces of things that supposedly meant something to you— a charm, a clock, an old car, a buggy, a bed, a cross.

All these pieces and remnants bring a sudden rush. With each stopping of the hologram, a rush or memory comes over you. The doctor, the lawyer, the nurse, the baker, the horseman, the blacksmith, the teacher, the Greek philosopher. You press past them all. Some of their visages almost seem to be fearful. Not because they were not you, but because they're long dead "you's." Memories are poignant, piercing, longing. Don't let yourself despair at this point, because it can rush at you. The futility of the one life dying on the battlefield—spilling your blood for what? Losing a child for what?

Press onward. Force yourself. Don't get caught in the despair. Lose your illness by tracking it: Is it in your liver, pancreas, chest, or heart? Drop it. It's part of the hologram. Forge past. Forge onward. Strengthen your will. Finally, you reach the portal doors.

As you turn around and face backward, there is no more debris. All those who were pathetic and needy, brilliant and possibly bad-motived, have been overcome. You climbed above them and got to the portals. As you get to them, there is a fresh, clean, lilac-scented wind. You realize that you have been tasting and smelling the rancidness of death and dying, aging and times past. It's old clothes littering now gone and blown away by the dust and the wind. Both portal doors swing open.

There you are in the presence of God. Your God, yourself, your God. Carrying with you the brilliant God-Consciousness as the avatars wished it to be. Grasping the hands of Mother and Father God, intellect and emotion. Despair is gone and loneliness dissipated. You feel the blessed relief of coming Home to the higher mind and knowing each time you get through, there will be less debris. Each time you turn around, more debris has disappeared, until finally, it's clean and sparkling. Even the cobblestones have no moss.

Bring yourself all the way up, feeling absolutely marvelous and rejuvenated, free from guilt, fear, agony, and pain. With quiet repose, come back to the you of now.

Specialness of Self

In trying to make your way through this world of bigotry and prejudice and inequalities, you've got to get away from feeling "special," and overcome the idea that the world "owes" you. Now, this has nothing to do with estimation of self. We will talk about that later, because that has to do with soul. "Specialness" has to do with the behavioral overcoat that so many of us wear when we are in life.

It goes something like this: "I deserve, I need, I must have, in order to make me happy, because I'm special." This is a very dangerous trap to your spirituality; it only lets you in for terrible disappointments. The "I Am" that comes directly from God is a different thing entirely. It has nothing to do with anything worldly.

You must neutralize such feelings by realizing that nothing attacks or can ever injure your definite, personal God. Listen to me very carefully: That's the one thing that can't be attacked or hurt, because you must not give God humanistic traits, and neither do you have that humanistic trait within your God-center to be hurt.

And yet, we see you going through crucifixion patterns every single day. You're crucified by your workers, and sometimes your children and your parents. You keep walking into these crucifixion patterns because of your "specialness." Sometimes this happens due to deep-rooted, wrong religious ideas that, "If you suffer more, God will love you more." No. Or, "God must love your child very much. That's why He took her." This makes an ominous false god.

If there is nothing else that Gnosticism tries to bring about, it is the reality of the true God.

If you look back on your life, you will find that your self-awareness really began to form at age 10. From there to about 18 or 19 is a very dangerous period. Think back to your preteen years. If you were told that you were short or fat or too tall or too ugly, such things began to take hold at that point. So if you thought of yourself at that point as stupid or fat or whatever else somebody called you, that stuck with you in what we call "the specialness of self." False specialness.

You're going to react defensively to anyone who treads upon that particular hurt point. That stops psychic and spiritual growth.

I would like for you all, when you go to bed at night, to really rinse through that area by saying, "From the age of 10 to 19, if there was any negativity that I've absorbed, I want to release it."

It helps if you can become less reactionary. That's so deadly. We find it so amazing that people will react when things are directed toward them, but not if it's toward a cause. A cause is what unites people. That's what creates religions, or helpful groups such as Mothers Against Drunk Driving (MADD). When people form together in a cause, the group creates strength. You come together with a God-center of one purpose to create a better good. What breaks apart a group is one person thinking they're more special than the other, rather than *surrendering*. You don't surrender yourself totally to another—that lands you in a cult. That's what happened in Waco, Texas. Instead, surrender to the unique god inside yourself, and forget all this external stuff.

Do I want you to go up on a mountain and sit cross-legged and meditate? No, but stop being so concerned about what comes to you or at you. It's so superficial. So many things are. It's like going through a jungle and having people shoot at you. It's terrible. But when you get out of the jungle, you're not going to walk around dodging bullets your whole life, are you? You must move forward.

What are "specialness" warning flags?

I will give you some perfect examples. A woman may say, "I've always been a good mother. I've done the best that I know how to be, and what did I get in return?"

There was no written guarantee. Instead, you should say, "I was a vehicle by which these entities came through. I did the best I knew how to do, and now they're on their way." That's tough, but it's true. And it's more realistic than taking personal responsibility for bringing a "good" or "bad" person into the world.

Another one is, "I've given him the best years of my life." How could you possibly make a judgment that those were the best years? Why didn't you look at it as being years in which you learned? And what about the fact that you charted it? It's all right to mourn what you might not have been able to have, but mourn for just a little while.

Wanting a nice companion, a wonderful little white house with a picket fence, and beautiful children playing in the yard who never pick your flowers and never say, "Shut up," and "I wish you were dead"—this can only be fulfilled in the movies.

How can we help our children through those formative years?

Go in with them at night and say their prayers with them. Or just surround them with the white light of the Holy Spirit. It's very good to do this for children, even when they're sleeping. Each night for a week, tell them to say, "I surround myself with the white light of the Holy Spirit. Any negativity that I've absorbed, let it be released, *right now,* into the light of God's love." These are wonderful words that will hit the soul. You can use them for yourself, too.

Can our guides help cleanse us?

Yes, if you've given them permission. You only have to do this once. But if you haven't given permission, we just stand outside and can't get in. In fact, I would make sure you do this every so often. It's very much like spring house cleaning.

Everything is accessible to us if you allow it. You must know that. But not if your guide feels that it would jeopardize your privacy. Of course, there is nothing you could do that we haven't seen or heard or done ourselves. So I don't want you walking around saying, "Oh, goodness, whatever I do is being discussed over on the Other Side."

CLEANSING MEDITATION

Put your hands upward on your thighs. Make yourself at peace. Bring your God Consciousness up right from the center. Identify with the spiritual masters who walked and talked and spread joy and love throughout the world. Bring the Mother God around you as Her mantle spreads out over you and blesses you with Her arms around you. Bring the Father God with His omnipotent grace as a sentinel figure that holds you, constantly giving, nonjudgmental, and static in emotion. And the Holy Spirit that moves throughout all these created forces, of which you're a part.

The uniqueness of your own created force begins to grow large. We will now divide the false specialness and cut it away from us like an iron maiden that has been around us. Let it be removed from you, this "I deserve, I need, I must have." You're impervious to the onslaught of conditioning. The words, which have been said from the time you were very young, now rinse away.

All the arrows that have struck you, all the words that have fallen, all the hurts that have befallen you, all the physical ills that you have sustained—all these rinse from you, leaving you clean. Your self-esteem, the God-center, rises up and gets rid of this reactionary illusion of the specialness of yourself. Let it fall away.

The reality of what you do deserve and what you will get

will come to you in only the most blessed, positive ways. Everything else then becomes an illusion. Life is an illusion, a dream, something that passes. It's the high pinnacle of emotion. Watch all the chaos go on below you. You're removed. You're in action but not reactionary.

You now move through life not expecting but accepting, allowing, passing through, nonhurtful. Don't live your life anymore with "ifs." Don't live your life anymore with "tries." Simply live straight, positive, immeasurably strong, and healthy.

Keep remembering, "You're not your body. That's only the car you're driving." Say to yourself that you will have respect for yourself and others. You will have discipline of your thoughts. That way you won't get phobic. The will and judgment center comes up so that you will control your thought, your mind. Release, release, release.

The white light of the Holy Spirit scours through. The guides may walk through today. They may visit, clean up, help, and be instrumental. Be watchful, be self-auditing, be aware.

As you protect a beautiful garden, protect your inner self. Because you're precious, more precious than you know to God. Because we are all fingers of the same hand. Feel the love of our blessed creator, Mother Azna, our blessed Father, our blessed God Consciousness, Jesus—the man who walked, and all the other prophets who walked. Ask for them to attend you. Ask for all the archetypes to come. All the people who have passed on from past lives and this life to attend you. Be still in your soul; be quiet and hear the Voice of God.

From time to time, people wonder what I looked like in life. In my life, I lived to be very old, and I was very proud of my age. In my younger days, I had very dark hair. I wore a very triangular turban; I didn't wear the usual Sikh turban. I was very bronzed of skin, with very large brown eyes, a very full mouth, a very flat nose, and a very strong chin.

I sound like I'm making myself better. The combination sounds good, but together it wasn't all that wonderful. I was very sturdily built. As I got older, I let my beard grow white. I was very furrowed, which I loved because it gave me a wise look. I let my mustache grow white and kept it, and my beard grew very long.

I began, in my specialness of myself, to fancy myself a wise man. I realized very early that I was falling into a false prophecy, which was my own. I was beginning to have a specialness of myself that wasn't true. I was more intent on the wisdom of my days that I thought were so like jewels. So you see, we all fall into the traps. Then when I realized I wasn't so special but that I was becoming so close to God, I didn't need that specialness anymore. I trimmed my beard and began to look more "normal."

I had a very round face. In your measurements, I imagine I would have been around 5'10" or 5'11"—very tall, I might add, for my day. I had dark skin and almost almond-shaped eyes. Even though my eyes were round, they slanted upwards at the side. Many people thought I was of Oriental or Asian heritage. I blended very well with the cultures because of that. But I was very proud of the darkness of my skin, because I loved the color. In fact, I think some of you are entirely too white.

The Challenge of Addictions

Francine: Psychological addictions can often be more ferocious than physiological ones. More often than not, the former leads to the latter. So if you think I'm just going to talk about alcohol or whatever, then listen carefully, because there is far more to it.

The physiological self, when you incarnate, becomes very dependent upon the Earth plane. Now it has a lot to do with the general and all-pervasive negativity of the earth's dominion, but it also has to do with the parenting process. This isn't to make any of you parents feel bad, but it's all-important to give to the child what it needs and what it wants.

So you come in as an infant, and what happens? With all well-meaning intent, and I don't want you to change this (I'm just showing you how it occurs), when you're hungry, you cry and you're fed. When you need entertainment, somebody entertains you. When you're bad and then you get good, then you're rewarded by what? A cookie.

All of a sudden you reach a certain age, and you're supposed to outgrow that. It's very hard because you're not only burdened with bodily needs, but you're burdened with the psychological needs. "I came to this earth. I came from the Other Side where everything is available, and it should be available now."

So you carry more of a mind-set with you than you could ever imagine. You're coming from a place where, if you want a beautiful building built, you *think* it into being. If you want a different visage, you *think* that into being. It's instantaneous. You get here in a physical body, and you can't understand the limitations. You were a baby who got everything you needed and wanted, but then you became an adult and still expect everything to be handed to you. You still think that somebody should nurture you, feed you, help you, cuddle you, and care for you. So you're always in a state of bereavement because you don't have everything you want, especially nurturing.

So from that, all of us become very addictive personalities. The addiction can be to another human being, a state of existence that we think we deserve, a state of health that we think we have earned, or a state of mind that we think should be possible. So we're constantly focusing, almost psychotically, on a certain mind-set. You will find that many people—even the best of you (myself included) tend to become almost single-focused on certain areas during life.

There isn't anyone that isn't addictive. You have to be addicted to life or you wouldn't have come down here. The danger zone is when the sustenance of life, the acquiring of things in life, and the pleasurable things in life begin to take over the higher mindedness for you in life—that is, when you don't realize that such things are very transient.

I don't want you to live like monks and nuns. That isn't what I'm saying. You can live in great luxury and still be impoverished in your soul.

Many, many years ago, Jesus taught that it does no good for someone to gain all the material possessions in the world, just to lose their soul. When I speak to you like this, I don't want you to feel that because you wanted the new dress, the new pair of pants, the new car, the new apartment, or the new drapes, that you're being bad. It's only when this becomes a focus of obsession.

You tend to become obsessive about all aspects of your life. Notice while you're sitting there what your major obsession seems to be. You will find it very quickly. When you become obsessive, you push the very thing away from you that you aspire to.

Obsession is a negative barrier. "I want my son to be so good," you say. "That's all I think about." You have now created a steel block. Unfortunately, you have also wound him into a karmic wheel with you. The other person catches it, links to you, and you link to them.

"Only if they get better, will I be better." You have set up a warp that keeps growing. We watch it ripple. You say, "But Francine, if I want it, wasn't it put there by my chart?" No. That's a fluke that appears from living in life. Your wants have nothing to do with your chart. If you never learn anything else, please realize that your wants are physiological in nature, and many times have nothing to do with your chart.

Emotion and intellect must coexist. The intellect, in this case, is where superior spirituality resides. Emotion climbs to it. Altruistic spirituality resides in the intellect.

Sometimes that gets inundated by the emotion of, "Why couldn't I have had a better child or a better marriage? Why am I alone? Why don't I get a better job? Why aren't my children better to me? Why do I feel neglected? Why am I rejected?"

That's an addiction. Instead, realize that you could walk this road truly alone (not that I recommend that). If everything else was taken away from you, you would walk it alone. Then you've ripped the addictions from you. Now, that's very hard. But it really is letting go of so much of the worldly things. Really think yourself into a state of aloneness. Not loneliness, but aloneness. Really program yourself.

If I said to any of you who are parents, "If you lost your children, what would you be? Could you go on?" Now, the cry goes up from the heart, "Probably, but I don't want to face that." Of course you feel that. I know. I watched my daughter being killed. Even though I'm on the Other Side, when I come into Sylvia's body, the grief comes back. Now I don't have that when I leave the body. But you see, even for the short time that I'm in, I'm subjected to the grief that was. The grief is similar to what still hangs in Earth's dominion.

That dusty day when the Conquistadores came in and stabbed my darling daughter comes back so real. I ran out to try to save her, and I took up the spear, also. That pain is still there. When I leave this body and go back Home, it's a vague memory. I think that's part of the reason why a lot of spirit guides don't choose to come into a body.

Pains and hurts from other lifetimes collect and hang in this world?

From every lifetime. But the good also does. As long as you *don't get addicted to the pain.* That's what this is about. Certainly all of you have been raped or drowned or murdered or tortured or any number of things. But haven't you all been artists and priests and healers and helpers and courtesans and great statespeople with great lives? But unfortunately, people get addicted to the pain. They don't get addicted to the glory, the light, the beauty.

We so often see people living painful lives and being in negative relationships, afraid to get out of it. They say, "Well, at least it's familiar."

The yearning to be popular—to be loved and accepted—is another obsessive, deadly trap. Do you know that one of the great teachers who tried to get rid of that was Buddha? Not only with his eightfold path, but he was the one who said, "Release things into the universe." To live with nature. To be compatible. That was what the Gnostics and Native Americans believed. To coincide with, blend with, work in harmony with. Not against. Not "I want." It should be what the Universe "wants." Get into "we, us, they," rather than "I."

If you really have faith and belief, instead of becoming obsessed about what you want, then you can achieve anything. Have you ever noticed that when you're conscious of your body all the time, everything bothers you? Or when you're dieting, all you think about is food. The minute somebody says they're going on a diet, they do nothing but think about their next meal. But if they were in love, they would never think about eating.

So never say to yourself, "I'm going to diet." Instead say, "I'm going to exercise, and I'm going to eat right."

Do we carry addictions to the Other Side?

Oh, no. It is only a physiological thing. We don't seem to carry any of that over. People spend so much time worried about their addictions. They get obsessed about whether they're addicted or not. But it only happens while incarnate.

Facing Ourselves

Sylvia: The following is a little excerpt from the Gospel of Thomas in the Gnostic Gospels:

> *Jesus said, "If you bring forth what is within you, what you bring forth will save you. If you don't bring forth what is within you, what you don't bring forth will destroy you."*

People who are not willing to face themselves are not willing to face truth. The Gnostic Gospels were found in 1945 at Nag Hammadi in upper Egypt, in a Coptic earthenware jar. These were the secret teachings and the Lost Gospels. Some scholars feel that it was Jesus' twin brother, Thomas, who actually wrote this about him.

When the church began to stray from the truth about God, the Gnostics kept these secret books full of love and wisdom and goodness hidden from the populace, knowing full well that we could be in jeopardy of—not our lives, but our writings and our teachings—as is still the case. Yet it's so plain and so simple and so beautiful, as Jesus had always wanted.

One of my people told me about a conversation she'd had with a Presbyterian minister. She asked, "What religion do you think Jesus was?" The minister hesitated for a minute and said, "Well, Christian." She said, "Couldn't be. *Christian* means 'follower of Christ.' Christianity came afterwards." The minister paused for a minute and he said, "By God, I think you're right."

Jesus was a Gnostic and an Essene—a seeker after truth—as are we. I'm like you. You're like me. We're all alike in that we want to find the kernel of truth. Sometimes the kernel that you find grows from a small acorn to a giant oak tree. That's what we must find: the whole.

We must rid the world of false concepts such as hellfire, damnation, and a vengeful god. Religion is to give hope, help, and a shoulder to cry on. Remember, what's hidden will destroy you.

Religion isn't just ritual. It should help us understand our daily lives. *Religion,* actually, if you look it up in the dictionary, means "a set of strongly held beliefs and values that people live by." It's closer to philosophy than ritual. Religion is a set of beliefs, not a bunch of rituals.

What we must have, in order to be a living, breathing religion, is right actions. We have to be willing to stand firm, and to give up all the old "stuff." Give up all the guilt and the hurts.

It doesn't matter how we come to God. Each one comes individually.

Consider this. On Mother's Day, each and every one of a certain mother's five children walks up to her and presents a different gift that they have made or bought. In her heart, she accepts these gifts with the loving knowledge that each gift is precious. You know the scene: the drawings that get pasted up on the refrigerator, or the little homemade ashtray that we all got—the clay one with all the little fingerprints on it that no mother would trade for her soul. Then imagine how you would feel being this mother, if all your kids went out into the front yard and fought about which present was the best. That's what religion has become.

We present ourselves before God in our own individual ways. Why have we lost our own dignity? Why have we become prejudiced? Why does one religion proclaim to be so much greater?

We want to be *spiritual*, not *religious*. We want to be searching, knowledgeable, caring, and loving. That's the core of it. We don't care what Episcopalians or Catholics do. Each and every one of us knows that those in their own church are presenting themselves as a child before their God, and so are we.

We want to be positive, but in seeking truth, we can't shy away from strife and negativity when we encounter them. We say this continually: You have to go all the way through a negative emotion before you come out on the other side with a positive emotion. If something or someone is aggravating you, then for God's sake, be angry and mad about it. Admit to yourself, right here and now, that you hate what this person has done. Then you're able to let it go, and then come back into the grace of loving.

We can't suppress those emotions. God gave them to us for a reason. We have all the human emotions such as grief, hostility, anger, and vengeance. That's part of life. Without those, we lack a rounded personality. Chances are that we have lived many lives to acquire them. The more lives we live, the more attributes we acquire. But we can also pick up more negatives. The negatives will rise just as high as the positives many times.

Francine was saying to me, "For everything we get, there must be a payback." That doesn't mean money. Sometimes it can, if you can give nothing else, but it also means time. We're all a community working together. We've got to give time back. We can't just take. We've got to be in service, because that's all that really means anything here—to be in service for each other and for our God-centeredness so that we ascend our highest selves back to where we came from.

Francine: Thus, a religion is started. People from all walks of life congregate together and find each other in miraculous ways. If you stop and wind your way back to how you came upon this church, it will be quite a miraculous tale.

The words *Novus Spiritus* bring about the creation of the "new spirit." We are really an old spirit, but we bring about the new spirit within the soul to revive the old—to bring about a greater understanding of the overall whole so that everyone, eventually, comes to their own salvation without fear.

What no one realizes is that Jesus never founded a church, ever. I don't care what church claims him—he never founded a church. He founded a community that was spiritual, that moved, that had ministers who administered to people. That's what the apostles were. They didn't have to tithe. No big, impressive churches were ever considered.

The further a church gets away from the people, the more rules that they put into effect. Think for yourself. Think about what's right and good—to get out and help other people. To love and be and fulfill a mission is far more spiritual than any rituals, dogma, or rules.

The only way you can ever tell if something is right is if your "gut feeling" tells you. Even if you walk away right now and never come back, you must listen to this part. It used to be that people didn't need to get involved unless they wanted to. You didn't always have to stop for an accident. You didn't always have to stop and do something for someone else, although that was always the universal law. But it didn't always bring with it the karma that it does now. If you don't turn and help each other now, then no battle will be won at this time. You will stay in a "dead time" zone, in which you can't hear the voices of God or your guide. You will continue to feel lost, sent into battle with a radio that's gone dead.

Each one of you is a karmic catalyst for each other, for your family. How many of you have emulated someone in the family or a close person? Sylvia had her grandmother. A karmic catalyst is someone who goes through things so that others can watch and experience with them. This is something that has to be done, tragically, during any fight for good. A person is either elected to the position or pushed into it. Unfortunately, karmic catalysts don't always finish right-side up. This time, what's right must end right-side up.

Can we call on Azna at such a time?

Yes. Mother God can intercept and create miracles. But that's something not charted. You or I can't create a miracle, but if enough people petition Her, She can. You can petition for as many things as you wish. You don't have to prioritize them.

But I think if you're going to ask for a miracle for all, ask for yourself, too. People often have a very hard time feeling worthy of getting a miracle for themselves. Everyone is entitled to a miracle, and many in a lifetime. It's only churches that have told you that you're not. No one is elevated over another.

Azna is coming around very strongly now. Everybody should be able to feel Her. She is mighty, rampaging, and powerful. When She eventually gathers Her groups around Her, She can really be strong. The earth has put Her to sleep for so many thousands of years, but She has always been here.

It's time for the female principle to be restored. This is a matriarchal movement. Sylvia speaks of that constantly. That certainly isn't to rule out the males, but we must have a balance.

Guilt vs. Compassion

Sylvia: I'm so sick and tired of guilt. The problem we have is to find something else in place of guilt. So many times with my clients, I've seen that if you remove guilt, they walk around empty. They don't know what to do without it. They want to fill it up with something. It's sort of like taking off a pair of tight shoes that you've worn for so long, and realizing that you can actually walk without pain.

Put the word *compassion* in the place of *guilt*. Compassion means "caring and understanding." It's not pity or empathy. It means, "I care by choice." You're not pulled down by a feeling of "I have to . . ."

As you probably know, the Essenes were Gnostics. The Essenes authored the Dead Sea Scrolls. Most theologians now say that these scrolls were definitely part of the original Bible, but church officials eradicated and ruled them out over time. In A.D. 325, during the First Council of Nicaea, they eliminated everything that had to do with reincarnation and eradicated the Gnostic movement.

The Bible, as we now know it, is not the full version of the Bible.

There was one passage that struck me as reflecting our philosophy so much: "An edict went out amongst the Essenes [later the Gnostics] that stated, 'Stop holding on. Quit having the stubbornness of guilt.'"

It really struck me how tenacious guilt is. We have to discern if we're on the right path, which means being in tune with God's will. You're the experiencing part of God feeding data back to the Divine. We have to discern what is righteous guilt, what is stubborn guilt, and what is inane guilt. If the motive, the heart, and the emotions are pure, they will weigh strongly in our defense.

Guilt is a killer—no doubt about it. Guilt causes cancer and breaks up families; it can make you crazy and make your soul weigh heavily. Now, we're a guilt-programmed society. We get it in our religious structures. Churches have been the biggest harbingers of guilt. Sometimes I just wonder if the guilt and negativity hasn't become its own Antichrist. It's something to think about.

Think about the fact that we have guilt about our children, and why do we? We're programmed socially, economically, and culturally to think that whatever goes wrong is our fault. No. You see, these entities come to us with their own written charts that they must fulfill. How much control do we really have over it? Very little.

Because you're human, you rant and rave over the fact that you have a kid who happens to be rotten, or your parents are driving you crazy. Let's take leave of all this screaming and yelling and hollering. If someone is sitting in front of me and I walk over and smack that person, I *should* have guilt, because that person hasn't done one single thing to hurt me. I should have guilt for that. See what I mean? That is an overt action against someone who hasn't done one singular thing to me in my life.

But let's say that someone comes up and hurts you, and you turn around and say to them, "Stop." Or you push them away with justifiable anger. You have so much guilt over things that you have no control over. Why? Because somebody told you that you were not a good enough mother, spouse, or child.

So you don't like your mother—well, maybe no one does; maybe she just isn't likable. Did you ever think of that? So you think your kid is rotten—that may very well be the consensus of 70 other people. Why do you have guilt? Do you think that because this entity came through you or you married this person, it's your responsibility forever and ever to take up that crucible?

Let me tell you from my own experience, my friends. In one twinkling of an eye, because of a belief, it can be taken away. How do you stand with that? You stand tall.

Overall this is only God, and the way we serve Him.

I would never ask you to do anything I haven't lived through and done. When you make that commitment to God, you can have it all. He may let it drop away or it may be taken, but what has anyone ever taken from you? Make sure that when all things are taken, you don't stubbornly hold on to this guilt. We hold on to that more tenaciously than we do any material thing.

Once I helped this woman's whole family: Her mother got off alcohol, and her brother got off drugs. Afterwards, she said to me, "Now what am *I* supposed to do?" She wanted to carry the responsibility and guilt for their limitations.

We don't like to let go of our old, familiar dragons. They breathe fire at night, and haunt our beds. We say, "Oh, there you are. I know you're there." Our anxieties and our illnesses are these feelings of guilt. Jesus was trying to rid us of this. Even the sacrament of baptism was originally meant to symbolically wash away what has gone on before in your past lives.

Please let go, and let your soul stand with dignity. How dare you not know that you're a spark of the Divine?

You're a spark of the Divine Mother and Father God. You're a beautiful, perfect, infinite soul. Don't let the world get you. Don't let the world put that on you. Walk above all of this. The sky won't fall in on you. *You* may fall in on you, but God's love, which is constant forever, will keep on pulling you out if you stick to your belief.

Little by little, from this seedling, grows a gigantic mighty oak
that gives shade and comfort, not hardship. We're not going to
chop down our mighty oak and build a wooden crucifix. We're
not going to go through any kind of mental cruelty or guilt cruci-
fixion pattern. So take it upon yourself to be part of this commu-
nity, this growing miracle. That's what you're witnessing here.
A growing miracle is beginning to take hold.

It's beginning to bud. It's beginning to bloom.
— Sylvia

One person, walking with the light, can enlighten many.
Light springs out. Strangely enough, many times it will
spring out of darkness. But light, coming from light
into darkness, makes it even more brilliant.
— Francine

I ask for the white light of the Holy Spirit to surround
and protect me. I will not be afraid. My God-center
will be intact. I will live only by my own truth.
— Sylvia

§ Chapter Three §

THE GREAT BATTLE

Francine: From the very beginning of Creation, certain entities wanted to gain more love, more knowledge, and more spirituality. There is a fine line, however, between the ones who want spiritual evolvement, and some of the flukes that occurred because of this. That's where you get a misinterpretation in the Bible. It's not a total misinterpretation, but it explains why a "Lucifer" was put into being. Some entities did become megalomaniacal and broke totally from the Godhead. You could construe them to be negative entities, almost in direct opposition to God.

These entities reside on *Noir;* this word means "dark or black." They manipulate large energy patterns. They can exert their power indirectly as a blockage from spirituality. They can't affect humanity when residing on the Other Side because they have no presence there. But the minute you enter life, you're in the battleground of light forces versus dark forces.

Rather than construct a "devil" with horns, which of course would be an untruth, I would like for you to view the "dark side" as a negative energy pattern. This vibrational level is in harmony with the incarnate vibrational level—and the dark forces have what you might call a "free-for-all" in your world. With their energy, their pattern fits into your economic structure. It fits into all types of stress. Any type of negativity that you could ever think of is manipulated by energy forces.

Once you're aware of the enemy and the form it takes, it can no longer be a threat to you. You may ask why God has allowed this type of vibrational level to enter the dominion of matter. The reason is that the negativity of the dark forces is set up as a test pattern. As a result, you're tested through many adversities. You knew full well before this life that you came in with a mission to gain your own spirituality over any type of dark energy force.

When you're being manipulated by dark energy forces, you will know it by the heavy and oppressive feeling you get. You may find that you're more aware of it at night. Night's darkness has always been the herald of dark entities. That's why your horror movies have "things that go bump in the night." If you're ever fearful of something being in your room or any energy force that you're not comfortable with, turn on a light or light a candle. But in all the years that I've been in consciousness, which is from the very beginning of time, just like you, I've never seen any force that can wreak havoc with a person except *their own force*. You don't need to be afraid of things that go bump in the night, as much as *your own* force going bump in the night.

When the oppressive feeling comes unbidden, and all of a sudden you feel this way, the energy force of the negativity has condensed in some way around you. You can dispel it with light. If you don't want to turn on an actual light or a night light, then visualize the white light.

What makes us responsive to manipulation?

False ego, by which I mean not having a true sense of the "I Am," but instead, having a desire to absorb manipulative qualities and power plays.

There are significant differences between people who are gray, people who can be manipulated, and dark entities. Any white entity can be manipulated, but usually snaps back onto track like a rubber band. Probably everyone has been manipulated by their own "gray forces," because of the vibrational level of this planet.

That's what I was talking about, the oppressive feeling. Not even heavy materialism gets you into gray. It's usually malicious forethought to create harm continually, and very few white-souled entities can keep that up for any length of time. Within the incarnate human being are all types and modes of vengeance, lying, rudeness, cruelty, ego—that certainly doesn't constitute a dark or even gray entity. It comes with the package of the physical vehicle. Most of these "sins" are short-lived. Very few entities can keep a hate campaign going continually. There are some very powerful white entities that incarnate, too. Whenever you have dark ones, you will have white ones come in as an almost total balance.

Dark entities are not usually parading around in public, as much as they're insidiously invading. If they were to be outwardly visible, most light entities would find them out immediately.

Negative thinking and emotions attract negativity to us?

Yes. It gives dark entities a breeding ground in your mind. I don't want to frighten you in any way, because it isn't frightening. It's often helpful to get someone more highly evolved than you are to pierce through that darkness and open it up.

Are the negative and positive forces equal?

No. God has always taken precedence. Always. There is no equality in that. The only thing is that in the dominion of the world's vibration, dark is stronger because this is their homeland. It's like we're fighting on a foreign battleground.

When a dot of white appears, a black dot begins to try to submerge it. You know what happens when you put black and white together? You get gray. That's what we have to fight. You must add enough white to turn that gray to white. You don't care about the dark soul. That's never going to change. All you have to do is survive over the dark.

Does God control the amount of negativity on this planet?

Yes. God wouldn't allow you to take more than you could bear. It's not factual for any human being to say, "I've taken more than I can bear." If you get to that point, you should verbalize it so that your own God-center can rise up and attach to the God without, to negate all negative forces. God's hand does steady all things.

Do children attract negative energy forces?

No. You're speaking of a child, and there is full protection of children. That's why it's so ridiculous to think of a child being possessed.

How can we fight against negativity?

Repeat as necessary, "I'm a child of God. I'm free of any darkness. I am liberated from any force of darkness. I'm a child of God. I've now accepted the God Consciousness and the power of Azna into my heart. My very being, right now, is illuminated in all areas."

Then, really start concentrating on your aura going out 30 to 60 feet. After that, it begins to dissipate, but that still covers a lot of room. If people did this on the highway, you would be very surprised at how you would minimize "road rage." If you have the kind of car, as some of you have, that seems to be pasted together by wishes and chewing gum, it will keep your car together. One thing about mechanical things, they're sentient. If you talk to your cars, toasters, and washing machines, they will have a longer life span. Everything has a molecular life force—not as we know it to be, but their own molecular force within that listens.

Raheim: Negative implants are very detrimental to your physiological system. It's something that you need to guard against. People will give each other negative implants by saying things that shouldn't be said. For instance, if I were to say to someone that they had a predisposition for tuberculosis, that immediately gives them a negative implant, true or not, that they must then work to reverse. It begins to take root in the subconscious. You must say, "I reject this."

Now that doesn't mean that you have to be overly cautious about the words you utter, because there is such a thing as fighting back, confrontation, and righteous anger. They're all part of the things that need to be said.

An ancient practice from early Sumeria, which is marvelously viable, is to put your index finger to your forehead over your third eye. Then, in your own mind, say, "I reject this negative implant through my third eye."

Next, put your index finger over your heart and say, "I reject this negative implant through my heart chakra." Those two are the most vulnerable chakras. Negativity goes through the third eye, blinds your psychic sense, and settles in your heart chakra. If you don't get rid of it there, it will go lower into your system.

Now, for example, let's say you get a negative review at work. Don't allow this negativity to implant you. When reading it, put your finger to your forehead. You don't immediately have to do this; be very unobtrusive. Make it seem as if you're rubbing your forehead. By doing so, you're taking charge of your own vehicle and blocking out that negative implant.

The simplest and most direct way to dispel attacks of negativity is to call on the Angels of Light. "Ask and ye shall receive," said Jesus. Call on the Warriors of Light. The problem that we have is getting you to ask. All the archangels and all the archetypes are waiting for your call, but they can't go into battle unless you ask. It's like an army ready to do battle, and no one blows the trumpet. It's so simple. Ask for your angels to attend thee.

Every day you should ask the archangels to protect you. Now, of course, you know of Raphael, Michael, and Ariel, but there are legions of white archangels. Legions.

All of us are capable of being white or dark?

Francine: There are some entities that have within them the option of turning dark or gray. Most entities have within them traces of gray, but not full darkness.

When we started out, we were much grayer. As we proceed through life, we get much lighter. But the attacking of self—yes, in essence it could be said that's when we let the gray take over and the dark thoughts come. But I don't want anyone to feel that they have the option to turn dark. If they were going to, they would have done so long ago.

How are dark entities different?

Oh, usually you have a vibrational feeling about them immediately. They're not just irritating, but there is something almost repellent about them.

What qualities do dark entities have?

They make commitments they can't keep. They play mind games. They're not steadfast. They say one thing and live another. They don't stick by their principles; they don't have many principles. They're in for their own comfort and their own power. They're tremendously into graft and greed. They will do anything to save their own skin. They're incapable of loving themselves or anyone else, but they make such a good show of it.

There is nothing anywhere in the world that you have to be scared of except humankind. That's the worst evil and the worst demon you will ever face. I'm sure that someone facing a serial killer felt that he was facing a true demon. That's real flesh and blood without a red suit on. Those are the dark entities.

Don't ever think that a baby can't come in as a dark entity. That's what people have a hard time with. Of all the things that we have a hard time understanding, it's a dark entity coming in as a baby. Now, what's strange is that white entities will come through dark parents, or vice versa. Sometimes your relatives are from a different place.

Can we send negative energy to dark entities?

In fact, you can; it's almost like they feed off it. You have to be careful. They absorb bad energy, and the more sent, the more they rise in power. It seems to be better if you just turn and move away from them. I don't see any reason to have to confront a dark entity.

Can we change a gray entity to light?

Well, in essence, that's why you're all trying to "up" your spirituality. Maybe you don't even know that's why. Exactly what is the spiritual aspect for? It really is, in essence, not only to find yourself and your God within and the God without, but to fight the battle against negativity.

If just one of you goes out of here and begins to light other lights, you've made a difference in the world. It only takes a handful of Spiritual Warriors to do great things.

Nowadays, people are not held in by structures as much. They're free-moving, loving God in their own way without fear. That's the way it should have always been—love of God, not fear of God.

When a person turns white, they turn instantly. When they turn dark, it takes longer. When you speak truth to a person, it doesn't take much more than a sentence. Sylvia has been told time and time again, "That one sentence you said to me did it."

It's often effective to say, "You will find your own truth within you. Your truth will now be released so that you will be able to see it."

Example Lives and Mission Lives

As we have discussed in previous books, all mission life entities originated on the white planet of Nuvo. However, there is more information that you should know.

Nuvo is quite different from the dark planet of insanity that you're on now. I also come from Nuvo. It's very Grecian in its architecture; it has obelisks; it's totally white. We have marvelous flowers that grow. We don't have the houses that people have on your Other Side, rather, we have marvelous domed edifices that can be either large and round, or very square. Most of them are adorned with birds on top. We have animals in abundance.

Now, close to Nuvo is a sister planet of white entities that carries with it the example lives; just as elevated, just as known to God as everything else is.

- Nuvo I is home to the mission life entities.
- Nuvo II is home to the example life entities.

The example life entities come into life, and their lives are terribly difficult due to the simple fact that they have to go through severe trials and tribulations. Usually their lives are made public, and they have no aloneness. They must suffer so that everyone on Earth and the Other Side can learn, "If they did it, so can I."

The mission life entities also suffer excruciatingly, but they know that they have a spiritual mission that they must accomplish. They are not happy unless they're doing something spiritual. It comes upon them at any age—they feel restless, and anxious to begin doing something significant. Whereas, on the other hand, an example life entity is always deeply involved with life, seeming to go through things that no one could ever surmount, and then dealing with it.

Now, it's important to know the difference, because some of you are example life entities and some of you are mission. The amazing thing is that they can change their course. That's why a mission or example life entity is so terribly hard to track by anyone, because they write their charts as they go. When they jump out with a parachute, they don't know whether it's going to open or not.

Your chart is gouged in by your own hands as you go. That isn't the way other white entities do it. Let's just speak of the white, because we're tired of the dark now. If we spend too much time on them, we'll be no different from those who want to make a big thing out of the "devil." The vast majority of other white entities, who don't come from Nuvo I or II, write their charts and their missions prior to incarnation.

The example life entity wants to fight injustice in court; wants to challenge the organizations that won't bend; won't take anything sitting down; are the first ones to point out an injustice; and choose to fight along with those dealing with injustice.

Mission life entities do very much the same thing, but they don't take on the same suffering. They're not publicly displayed. They certainly save a lot of souls and do it within their families, and then spread out in larger circles. They really feel uneasy with life until they embark upon a spiritual quest of some type.

Many of you are currently in an "option life." I don't know the precise count, but the dark is no longer spreading, for the first time that anyone knows of. It seems that we have finally turned the tide.

The Battle

Now, speaking of the white entities, which you are, I've learned that many of you are also warriors; your lights have actually become brighter. There is an amazing, equal, and opposing phenomenon that we have never seen before: The dark has gotten darker. In all the eons of time that the Akashic Records show us, we can't find any precedent for this.

We even went to other planetary systems to see if any planet had ever turned this dark or this light. We're beginning to believe that there is more to this than we even know, because we're seeing Nuvoites coming in by droves. They're taking the position of your guides. It's almost like a group of tremendous warriors are coming in.

Based on what we've learned, I believe that this planet has become a pawn in the gigantic scheme of things, far beyond anything that any of us have ever realized. What happens here impacts the whole universe.

What I've been told is, "As this planet goes, so goes the chain of events throughout the whole universe." That to me means that unless you get the spleen taken care of, it poisons the whole body. So in the spectrum of God's plan, this must be one of the pivotal battles. What you're amassing around you now are tremendous numbers of onlookers. Extraterrestrials are now observing what's going on with all the white entities—how they're sustaining themselves, how they're holding up, and how they're battling this.

I don't want you to be afraid of the dark entities. They truly can give white entities a lot of hell, but they can't pull you down or physically harm you. Your strength will be fortified by the Nuvoites. We're even finding now that the guides are being fortified. There is a glorious entity named Bernadette who's been teaching me about this; she seems to be very close to Azna. She is very powerful, very beautiful, very warriorlike, and she is convinced that this planet will be won.

"This planet was made," Bernadette said, "to be the antithesis of everything that has ever happened anywhere." I've often told you that this planet was the insane asylum of the universe, but I didn't realize how far-reaching that was. It has become like a giant test.

From this, Bernadette says, the true warriors of the universe will then be picked. They will go to the Other Side, or whichever Other Side they're from. Or they can choose to go to other planetary systems and be like Bernadette or some of the other entities, which have come down from Nuvo. So as it stands now, not only are you fighting for your soul's perfection, but you're also elevating yourself to the level of a warrior and a teacher.

That would explain why so many spirit guides of white entities have reported to me that their loved one has said at one time or another, "I knew that I was destined for things far beyond what life seemed to offer me." They said this in trepidation, because that sounds like ego—but it isn't.

This is so much Azna's planet. This has been so much Her "baby." That bestows a special blessing upon those who rise up and fight. That may be why your dreams have been so disturbed at night, why you have been so restless and felt so many visitations; why depression hits you at odd times. Don't you see? It's because you're fighting on so many levels. These levels are on superconscious, as well as lower conscious, levels. This is the price you pay for becoming more spiritual, for your intuition and psychic ability coming up higher.

This is an evolving universe, an evolving perfection.
God, Himself and Herself, is a constantly growing
and evolving entity—perfect in Its evolving,
but nevertheless growing each day.
— Francine

Francine: Your strength will grow just as high. Be attentive and watchful now. You must be prepared to stand.

People will eventually negate themselves, and not by anything you do. The negativity that they exude won't be able to stand your light. It hurts, because, you see, your goal is to pull them toward the light. You will find that many drop by the wayside, even those you think you know well. But the love of God and the tenacity of your own soul will come forward.

Validate anything you hear by what you feel inside, in your solar plexus. That's the only validation.

As you grow spiritually, be very careful not to judge others.

Never forget that everyone has a spark of the Divine within them. Be patient and tolerant with those who are evolving. That certainly doesn't demean your evolvement toward spirituality. But be very, very careful of your own spiritual ostentatiousness as far as feeling that you're totally perfect. You must be very careful of that. If you feel that you can't learn from anyone anymore, and you think you have arrived, you're on dangerous ground. That isn't to slap your hands; it happens to all those who live physical lives.

Remember that if you were totally perfect, you wouldn't be here; you wouldn't suffer. You must always say, "I'm *evolving*," and never say, "I have evolved," because even when you go to your Home where I reside, you can never say you have totally made it. I haven't made it. Possibly we will *never* make it totally.

The fun is in the search. The greatness is in the journey. Even Jesus said that He was still evolving. Not to be pessimistic, but we must be realistic. Your life isn't going to become any easier. You can handle it one way or the other. You can become terribly emotional about it, or you can activate upon it. Emotions in this world are getting higher and higher. The things that you have to deal with are becoming more difficult.

How should we concentrate our energies?

The energies you're supposed to be dealing with are really not that complex. I find it amazing that everybody tries to make it that way. It's nothing more than giving of yourself and your love and ministering to people. That's where it is.

If you look back through time and learn about history, you will find that every time the white entities came together and the Gnostic groups started, the Mother God was very prevalent. This was in the time of Isis, the Babylonian period. Every single time it was split apart.

The Origin of Dark Entities

I know that we have talked about the fact that we always existed within God. I think that we're now advanced enough so that I can talk to you about the evolvement of humankind. This will explain a lot to you, regarding the darkness versus the light.

As I always say, there was no "beginning," but our first mode of existence was what we call the "state of voices." When we were all created, we were just voices, each individual. We waited patiently until the Creator gave us form. In essence, to have a voice, we had to have a mind that was, you might say, a singular cell of the Great Divine.

Now, you know that within your own mind, there are voices—there are certain synaptic impulses that resonate to certain things. Magnify this countless billions of times, and you will get an individual resonance. You all resonate to a different tone. That tone is your voice, your essence.

Some entities, about one-third of the billions created for this planet, wouldn't wait for God's hand to give them form. They wouldn't wait for the Creator's blessing, thinking they were better, they had more power, and they could come into life by their own force, which they did. This is where the darkness started, with those who put their will before God's will.

The rest of us waited until there was an "Adam" signifying all males, and an "Eve" symbolizing all females to come into life. That meant that Mother God had prepared a place for us. It was hard for us to be patient until then, because once we knew we had a journey to complete, we all wanted to begin.

The dark entities were very much like children who "know" better, run ahead of their parents, and do not listen to wiser counsel. It's like the old adage that so many of you know: "If you don't listen, you have to learn." For as long as the dark entities are incarnate on planets, they are separate from the light of Creation, due to their own egos.

Did they know what they were doing?

Absolutely. That's what makes it so abominable. As we've always said, motivation is everything. The motive separates good actions from bad. As perfect as any group can be, as perfect as God's Creation was, you see how selfish the human condition can be, taking more than is rightfully yours.

So you see that free will always existed, for both light and dark, and when we descended is when an ego-consciousness, an "I Am" consciousness, developed. That's when the schism appeared. The dark entities claim to be better than God.

Were these rebellious entities meant to go awry? I'm sure that they were, because there has to be an antithesis for anything good. It's uncanny how mythology bears this up. In every myth, a rebellion takes place in the heavens. There is always a good god fighting a bad god.

God, in ultimate wisdom (when I speak of God now, please know that I'm speaking in the plural—being emotion and intellect), said, "Let them (the dark entities) play it out. Let them have their sole reward in physical life. They wanted it very badly, let them have it."

So that's why they keep rotating into this planet, and are never allowed to go to the Other Side. Eventually in the "final" time (if there is such a thing as "final")—or in the ultimate time when this planet's use is finished, I'm told by the Council that God will absorb the dark entities into the Uncreated Mass to be purified.

Planet Earth is their domain; they excel and exceed and are dominant and strong in a negative sense. One of the greatest flaws of humankind is ignorance. To be ignorant means to be separate from enlightenment. That's why in your world you have bigotry and judgment and all kinds of horror.

Did they have a leader?

No, and they never will. But they planned to enter early, grab all the valuables before anybody got there, and gain all the profits.

I'm told that about 2,400 were really the initiators, and then the rest followed.

This sounds like greed.

Oh, absolutely. I've always told you that at the heart of any wrong, you will find greed. It's the core. Sift anything evil down to its lowest denominator, and you will find greed at its heart. They were greedy to gain the riches of the world.

Without dark entities, how would we have progressed and experienced for God?

That's a very, very good question. We've often brought that up in our theological studies, and we're convinced that it almost had to be. Otherwise, there never would have been anything to challenge your soul. Then the question comes up, "Were those people preordained? Were they sacrificed to do this?" No. I'm sure there would have been other tests.

Can we judge the darkness?

Oh, we can judge darkness. Don't ever think that we can't, *and we must*. However, the crucial difference is that we *must* stand firm in judging the *actions* of darkness, but never the *soul* of the individual entity acting.

Can we hear the tones of plants?

Yes, you can hear the tones of trees. I will tell you how you hear it. We have phrases, when we're in life, like "my soul sings." Other than smell, nothing stimulates memory like a song does. You will fit your life pattern into what was happening to you at the time that a song came out. This is shown in some of the research regarding people with severe Alzheimer's. When certain songs are played, their memory of that time will open.

When you eventually come over, you should go back and scan what we were like in the state of voices. It's quite beautiful. I just went in today and I've heard it many times, but I wanted to reaffirm my memory. At first it sounds like chimes, different resonance of chimes. Then, along with the chimes, came lights. Each person resonating their life force, pulsating. It was quite lovely. What is amazing, when you stand there in this myriad of lights and sound, you know exactly where your singular resonance is. You can distinguish yourself out of billions.

Where is the Hall of Chimes?

If you want to know exactly where it is in our geographical layout, it's behind the Towers. We can go in and it looks like a gigantic cathedral. When we go in, we can stand still and the whole area dissolves. We can look up and see all the chimes. We call it the "Hall of Chimes."

Now, when we first took a form, when we descended from our "star-chime," we looked androgynous. Then we began to form what we wished to be. That's when we decided to be male or female. That's when we grabbed what our theme was, what we were going to perfect for God. Up until that point, we were just sort of happy, baby chimes.

MEDITATION IN THE HALL OF CHIMES

Put your hands upward, and close your eyes. I want you to create a tunnel for yourself. Make it very broad and white. Don't be afraid that you could die. You're not ready. You should do this intermittently anyway. It will certainly prepare you for the journey when you finally come to it. The tunnel is very broad and white, and when you come through the tunnel, it pulsates. It seems as if the walls of the tunnel glow with almost a golden color, brilliant white at first.

You may be aware that as you push yourself through this tunnel coming to my side that you might be met by different entities, or people you have a sense of or a feeling about, who come close. We're all so anxious to meet anyway. Take yourself to the very end of this tunnel, and cross a bridge that looks like marble, under which a brook flows. Don't be afraid if you see people staring at you oddly. Just keep on walking. The grass is very beautiful. Please notice the color around you.

Don't be afraid if you're beginning to feel a little light-headed. You're displacing your essence a little bit. It's what the ancients called "astral mind travel." You're still in the body, still conscious of where your body is. Feel yourself traveling now. You can walk with a friend if you wish, or a guide or guardian; a guardian will come up anyway to make sure you get back.

Walk by the Hall of Wisdom, a big, domed building on your left. You can speed it up, because it's a little bit of a distance to the Towers. So very quickly we think ourselves to the Tower. Synergistically we can walk around the Towers now. Look at the Towers. They're very beautiful, spiraling.

Then all of a sudden you find yourself facing a beautiful cathedral—huge and magnificent, bigger than St. Peter's or any place you have ever been. But there is something very familiar about the carved doors and the big golden handles. Just so you can get your bearings, right behind you are the Towers. To the left is the Hall of Records, so at least you have a geographical bearing. The doors swing open. Go in by yourself.

The marble that you're standing on is such pure white; it isn't blinding, but there isn't a fleck, not a speck. It's the whitest white you have ever seen or felt. Now, all of a sudden you're going to begin to feel your surroundings. You feel the walls, the pillars, the color, or absence of it. You begin to think color. This is where synergism starts: If you want the pillars to be emerald green, they will be. If you want the walls on the side to be magenta, then they literally vibrate with that color.

All of a sudden, way far off in the distance, you begin to hear the very faint sound, your sound. You're compelled to look upward. It looks like a velvet night sky, and the sound rises in your soul. Let us call it the embryo or essence that was you, which is still there. It's like looking at a picture album. That embryonic sound and vibration was you then, and it is you now. You feel the infinity of your soul, the continuation of your life force from the very beginnings of your being, until now, and forever after.

You feel the beautiful, velvet darkness of the sky, and the color that permeates through your soul. That's your aura. You feel the tone that you carry in your soul. Feel the tone-chime, the music, the color, and your vibration. As you do so, feel how healed you are, how healthy, how totally in control you are of your destiny. Not false pride, but the pride of the soul that you have come this far.

Look at the infinity of all the other "starlets," the embryos of all souls created. The beauty that they gave out. Then look down that long hallway of memory and see how sometimes your chime dulled, went flat, discordant, or was silent. How your color dimmed, got dark, got brighter. How your vibrations slowed, slugged along, went fast, but is now steady. Steady and stalwart as the strongest heartbeat. Even more important, it's beating with the tone that's Mother and Father God. You're in sync with Their tones. Your vibration is in perfect harmony. You're in perfect harmony with the universe, all living things, all animals and plants, everything that moves on your side and mine. You feel the resonance, the call, the true voice of God; your own private tone.

You may go there as many times as you wish. I would advise you to go there for healing. If you have someone who *is ill, take them to this place. If they won't go, take them in your mind. Take all the people you love, even yourself. Take people who have passed. Reach out your hand. They will come with you to the Hall of Chimes. Feel how magnificent God's love is. Each chord, each color, each vibration, is individual. Think of the majestic intellect that created this. How fantastic. How absolutely magnificent.*

Feel yourself now walking out, carrying with you your own tone. If you don't know what your tone is, ask God at night to resonate this tone. From now on, don't go to bed without asking for the tone in your soul to be readjusted; almost like you would tune a piano—to make the tone perfect, to make the color as bright as it can be.

Bring yourself out. Go back to of the Hall of Wisdom. Don't get too homesick—you will be here sooner than later. As you come back across the bridge, and back down through the tunnel, become aware of yourself and those who traveled with you. Grab their hands, run, shout, scream, do whatever you want to do. Run with vigor. Run with renewed energy, as you did when you were five or six. Come all the way back to yourself.

Negativity

Sylvia: I want to discuss the Gnostic Gospels with you, which are actually some of the lost books of the New Testament. They're the truest part of the Bible.

They were never allowed in because they cramped the orthodoxy's power by saying, "Let us be as a commune. Give everything up, and we will share equally." The texts that were left out give love and compassion and understanding and sanction to life. The following is from the Book of James:

Our Lord said, "Once again I urge you. I'm appearing to you, and building a house that's very useful to you. You can find shelter in it, and it will remain standing beside your neighbor's house when their house threatens to collapse. I tell you the truth from knowledge and wisdom. Woe to those for whom I was sent down. Blessed are those who ascend to the Father.

"Again I admonish you, you who exist, be like those who don't exist, that you may dwell with those who don't exist."

Meaning, of course, those who have passed on. He continues:

"Don't let the Kingdom of Heaven become a desert within you. Don't be proud because of the light that brings enlightenment. Rather act toward yourself as I also acted toward you, because I came down to give knowledge to you."

Peter responded to these comments and said, "Lord, sometimes you urge us on toward the Kingdom of Heaven, but other times you turn us away. Sometimes you encourage us and draw us toward faith, and other times you draw us toward knowledge. But at other times you seem to throw us out of the Kingdom of Heaven."

The Lord answered and said to them, "I've presented you with knowledge many times. And James, I've revealed myself and my words to you, but you don't understand and you don't know. Now again, I see that often you're happy. Yet, although you're delighted about the promise of life, you're always so sad and gloomy when you are taught about the Kingdom.

"Nevertheless, you have received life through knowledge, so ignore words of rejection whenever you hear them. But when you hear about the promise and the knowledge of the promise, rejoice all the more. I tell you the truth: Whoever receives the life and believes in the kingdom that will come, will never leave the kingdom. This is all that I'm going to tell you."

Can you see how Jesus is getting cranky with this whole thing?

"Now, I shall ascend to the place from which I came. When I was eager to go, you drove me out. Instead of escorting me, you pursued me. Be attentive to the glory that's awaiting you. When you have opened your hearts and you have gotten rid of all the gloominess, you will listen and hear the hymns that await you in heaven."

The other day in the group, we were reading about negativity and there was a marvelous quote—"You don't have the right to be negative. Thoughts are things."

Even though our charts have been written, it's how we get through them that makes all the difference in the world. That's the difference between someone who can go through horrendous things and seems to make it all right, and somebody else who gets a hangnail and falls over. It's because those who really can make it through realize that all this is passing.

We really don't have the right to be gloomy and miserable and hateful, but we're also perfectly able to have dignity within ourselves. Dignity and pride of accomplishment and the manner in which we conduct ourselves—those are all exterior things that reflect the soul. If a person by their demeanor doesn't stand up tall, slumps, and even lets themselves go, this is an extension of what's happening internally.

Begin to stand tall and smile. The mind is a marvelous thing. If we act happy and sparkly and free of care, the mind and soul begin to say, "Well, everything must be okay." But sit around as a lump and don't move, and the mind says, "Well, they're dead," and so the body acts accordingly.

As we grow, we see the larger picture. So you have a pain in your leg—drag it behind you, but make the most of it. It's so easy to be grumpy, so easy to backbite and gossip about others, so easy to condemn. Until you walk a mile in a person's shoes, you don't have the right to say one word against them. Maybe we don't like the cards in our hand, but we ourselves dealt them.

It's easy to blame God, isn't it? That has always been the easiest target. I'm sorry, my friends. You dealt it, and you have to play it out. But I think there is a wonderful security in that, because you're smart. You knew what you needed while on the Other Side, and you plan your life to ensure that you challenge your soul accordingly.

Did you ever wonder what the word *salvation* really means? It's taken from the word *save*. Saving yourself to get back home intact, not just due to your belief in God or the Holy Spirit. It doesn't matter if you believe in God, because God believes in you.

Just focus on right actions. Take pride in accomplishment. There is no sin in pride, if you really did something good. And if you feel that you could have done it better, then perhaps you will. We're here to experience and learn. Don't be trapped by guilt if you've made a mistake.

Why not for one single day try to put yourself in somebody else's shoes, perhaps the very person you are having such a problem with? For one day, think and feel what it's like to be them. You may get a different perspective.

I want to share with you the following beautiful passage, which is the origin of the phrase, "If you're like children." It's from the Book of Thomas:

> *Jesus saw some babies nursing, and He said to his disciples, "These nursing babies are like those who enter the Kingdom." They said to him, "Then shall we enter the Kingdom as babies?"*
>
> *Jesus answered them, "When you make the two into one. When you make the inner like the outer, and the outer like the inner, and the upper like the lower, and when you make male and female into a single one, so that the male won't be a male, and the female won't be female. When an eye replaces an eye, a hand replaces a hand, a foot replaces a foot, and an image replaces an image, then you will enter the Kingdom. I will choose you, one from a thousand and two from ten thousand, and they will stand as a single one."*

Kingdom, above, refers to the kingdom of yourself. When you know yourself, you know the all—the male *and* female part. Does that mean we have to become androgynous? No. It means the left and right side of the brain must become united. When we do this, we become psychic. We become infused.

Emotion is our most beautiful asset, and our worst liability. Overcome fear: You have to love yourself. Since you're a child of the Mother and the Father, to not love yourself is like not loving God.

Unconditional Love—An Exercise

I want you to make a pact with yourself. For one week, I want you to love everyone around you. Now there's a catch to this: *Don't open your mouth about one single thing you want them to do.* I've done this with my family. I didn't open my mouth for one week. More important, don't ask anyone to do anything that you think they should, including yourself.

For one solid week, don't say, "I should do." This is an exercise in unconditional love, which means, "I love you because you exist in this world. That's all I ask of you, and I take joy in the fact that you exist." It's even hard by ourselves, but especially when we live with others.

I'm talking about not saying things like,"Wear the plaid shirt instead," or "Close the door so the draft doesn't get in." Don't say a word. This even includes young children. You may say, "Well, they will run rampant. They will tear up my house." But you will be very amazed at what a learning experience this will be, for you and for them.

We don't realize how much we drain each other's energy by manipulating others, when we could be giving to God and our own spirituality. Our goal isn't just to give unconditional love. We want to *be* unconditional love.

Francine: Please be very wary of one thing regarding unconditional love: Should you feel it or those who treat you badly? Yes,
but it's crucial to understand that unconditional love means loving
their soul, which is possible from a distance. You *don't* have to like
their actions one bit. This means that you do not have to put up
with them. Please realize that in situations where harm or abuse is
present, it's better to get yourself *out* of the situation. That's where
this concept got so far off base—you were supposed to "love your
enemies," but no one ever suggested that you should let them hurt
you. That's ridiculous. That isn't loving yourself. That's misguided
humility.

Is unconditional love always returned?

No. That's the hardest test of all. The cruelest discovery is to
find out that the people you think are the nearest and dearest to
you don't love you unconditionally at all. Their love relates to what
you can do for them financially, what you can give them, or how
you make them feel. The purest unconditional love we see in your
world is a mother's love for their child.

You may feel that the unconditional love that you have given
to such a person has been wasted, but in fact, your love has gone
somewhere. It may not have hit the target that you wished, but love,
like energy, is never lost. Someone, somewhere, gets hit with it.
Have you ever been going down the road, and all of a sudden you
get this marvelous sense of well-being? Chances are that you happened to walk into a stream of loving energy.

Hypocrisy

Sylvia: Hypocrisy is living a lie, it creates a split in your nature.
People should not proclaim being one way, and then live their lives
in another way. No matter who you are—a politician, a janitor, a
televangelist, or a member of Novus Spiritus—you can't say one

thing and do something else. All of you are ministers, not just my ordained ministers here. Every time you come to this church and go out and tell other people and bring people in or you try to relieve guilt and hatred, you are ministering.

Let's start at the family level. How good can I be as a minister if I can't take care of my own? If I cannot be a good daughter, mother, wife, friend, worker, or employer, then how can I expect to be a good minister? You have to think of those aspects in your life. Sincerity should be part of our everyday life and actions.

The right and left brain must be joined together at all times. Don't let the emotional side of your brain overwhelm you into flares of ego. We must assess what we really are. So we have a temper, we have a cranky side, we get despondent at times, and we get depressed and mad. All those things are normal when in human form.

You must not be the type of marriage partners who, in front of everyone, are all "kissy, kissy, kissy," and then go home and beat the hell out of each other. No. It's not right. Or a mother who physically abuses her kids—although I don't believe in passive rearing, either. Whoever said that you couldn't place a well-intended hand on the bottom of a kid? That isn't child abuse. We rush from one extreme to the other.

"What you see is what you get" might not please everyone, but it's a lot better than trying to live a lie. We must work through the stereotypes we're bombarded with, and put them behind us. The wondrous thing, which God has given us, is that we're flowers, and each one of us is different. Some of us are sunflowers, and some are pansies, dandelions, or roses. It doesn't matter—in a garden you need every single one of those flowers. *That's how you get color and light and beauty.*

So stand up for what you believe in. Whether it's Gnosticism or, more important, yourself. When all is said and done, that's all you have left. *You and your God-center.* That's all you will take Home.

Hypocrisy goes along with ingratitude, which is terrible. Once you practice hypocrisy, you also lose gratitude and you don't have loyalty. Be grateful to yourself for what you have done in your life. Say, "I love myself with all my faults, as well as for my good qualities. I might not like the flaws, but I'm working to make them better." Pat yourself on the back for choosing to hear this ancient truth and walking with God toward your own spirituality.

ॐ ॐ ॐ

I don't want to save you. I want you to save you.
— Sylvia

ॐ ॐ ॐ

91ST PSALM

He that dwelleth in the secret place of the most High shall abide under the shadow of the Almighty.

I will say of the Lord, He is my refuge and my fortress; my God; in Him will I trust.

Surely He shall deliver thee from the snare of the fowler, and from the noisome pestilence.

He shall cover thee with His feathers, and under His wings shalt thou trust: His truth shall be thy shield and buckler.

Thou shalt not be afraid for the terror by night; nor for the arrow that flieth by day;

Nor for the pestilence that walketh in darkness; nor for the destruction that wasteth at noonday.

A thousand shall fall at thy side, and ten thousand at thy right hand; but it shall not come nigh thee.

Only with thine eyes shalt thou behold and see the reward of the wicked.

Because thou hast made the Lord, which is my refuge, even the most High, thy habitation;

There shall no evil befall thee, neither shall any plague come nigh thy dwelling.

For He shall give His angels charge over thee, to keep thee in all thy ways.

They shall bear thee up in their hands, lest thou dash thy foot against a stone.

Thou shalt tread upon the lion and adder; the young lion and the dragon shalt thou trample under feet.

Because He hath set His love upon me, therefore will I deliver Him; I will set Him on High, because He hath known my name.

He shall call upon me, and I will answer Him; I will be with Him in trouble; I will deliver Him, and honor Him.

With long life will I satisfy Him, and show Him my salvation.

Chapter Four

MYSTICAL TRAVELER

Francine: In the "beginning," from the very inception of Creation's "always-ness," many of you chose to be what's called a *mystical traveler,* which is a soul that petitions to go on missions for God. Additionally, some entities petitioned later to become Mystical Travelers. The problem is that most of you don't know what to petition for. If you ask to become a Mystical Traveler, be very careful that you're aware in your heart of exactly what that means, which I will describe to you.

There have been many Mystical Travelers on this planet. There are too many to enumerate, but I will mention a few notables: Jesus, Shakespeare, Edison, Einstein, Nicholas Rourke, Joseph Campbell, Kahlil Gibran, Kierkegaard. Mystical travelers are not always messiahs or even well known, of course. They're pivotal souls who create a greater known good, like a catalyst. Stephen Hawking, a wheelchair-bound astronomer and physicist who has deep theories on the black holes, is a Mystical Traveler, too.

Mystical Travelers are almost like ministers in training. But instead of learning from leaders of any church, they're ascending toward God along their own path. A Mystical Traveler makes a covenant with God to be a teacher and a helper for humanity. In taking this upon yourself, you give your will over to God, agreeing that you will be a servant of God at any point. You actually then become part of Azna's Inner Court of Spiritual Warriors.

When a person asks for this mantle to drop, they're imbued with power and put into the light of knowledge. Once it's asked from the heart, without ego or pride but with some humility, the mantle does drop, never to be removed. Mystical Travelers become literal champions—saving planets, helping wherever they're needed, and becoming figureheads in life. For examples, consider Joan of Arc or Siddhartha Gautama, the Buddha. Many times they're martyred or hurt, and they're almost necessarily alone, all for the glory of God.

If you choose to be a Mystical Traveler and your twin soul doesn't, you must leave that soulmate behind. Of course, you might feel sad about that, but on the Other Side, there is no sadness. Do you ever come back and join with your loved ones? Yes, but you're always "on call" for any emergency in the universe.

At any given point, the world may need to be put back on track. You see, the world has its own pattern of evolvement. It's very much like how your own charts can be altered in minor ways; for instance, a car accident could be a fender-bender instead of a head-on collision, as Sylvia always says. When the world's events start to get unbalanced, then the Mystical Traveler is called upon to put the evolvement back on track. It's a great responsibility, but the benefits are blessings of purity, sanctity, great intelligence, and a swift passing Home.

There is a counterpart within the dark forces, as is so often the case, which they call their dark emissaries. Mystical Travelers must encounter many of these face-to-face.

How do Mystical Travelers differ from mission life entities?

Mystical Travelers are much more advanced. Mission entities are already included within the evolvement scheme. The Mystical Traveler goes down singularly as the need arises and brings order to an off-balance situation.

Can we switch back and forth in our lives?

A mission life entity can choose to become a Mystical Traveler. The Mystical Traveler always makes a sizable mark on history, while a mission life entity might just come in and form a group that pushes forward, which is just as important as making a large mark.

Every Mystical Traveler feels distraught at times. As the soul magnifies, the body can't hold it that well. Since Mystical Travelers have been through many lifetimes, traveling and learning, they have a wealth of knowledge, and it becomes very frustrating to fight the ignorance here. They always want to scream out, "Please. Don't you see it? It's just as clear as the nose on your face."

They walk a road alone. They, as well as the mission life entities, will incarnate if the project is big enough; then they will align together. It's like the warrior who walks alone until his army unit comes charging over the hill.

Were there any Mystical Travelers in Mexican history?

Yes, Quetzalcoatl. There were also many in the shamanistic Native American tribes, which are very similar to the Aztecs or Mayas or Incas. It all transpired early, even in early Sumeria and Babylonia. The Gnostic religion was rampant in those ancient cultures.

Can one make a false declaration to be a Mystical Traveler?

Mystical Travelers don't have that problem. Let's say that somebody joins us and they all of a sudden decide, "That sounds good. I think I will be one of those." No. They may say it, but they won't last. To say you're "Christian" and you don't live by it, you're not. They drop away. They never had the mantle in the first place, because you cannot fool God.

The Mystical Traveler is imbued with eight golden keys. These keys carry with them great and wondrous knowledge. Can all of you aspire to the eight golden keys without being a Mystical Traveler?

THE NATURE OF GOOD AND EVIL

Absolutely. You would anyway. Once you attain the eight golden keys, you may be able to explain them to people, but you can't give your keys away. Does that make any sense? They're your own. In other words, you're not able to turn around and sanctify another person. The eight golden keys are:

- Fortitude
- Loyalty
- Gratitude
- Psychic ability

- Mercy
- Honor
- Levity
- Great and grand intelligence

Let us discuss just a few of these. **Fortitude** takes in the strength of character and strength of soul, and stamina that far outweighs anything that most human beings can do. The ability to see straight ahead so people have the capacity and the strength of their bodies and wills to go forward.

Mercy may seem like a very strange key, but these individuals have unbounded mercy for everyone, sometimes to their own undoing. The mercy that the Mystical Traveler shows, with this tremendous knowledge and fortitude and loyalty and all the insights, the mercy then begins to spread wider. It encompasses so much of the nonjudgmental facets of life.

Mercy seems to allow us to be stepped on.

It means giving. You're afraid you will be stepped on by giving? Well then, you ought to look at Sylvia's life. If you're stepped on, you really spring back very easily. Mercy is probably one of the most beautiful of all the keys, and I don't know why you want to modify that. Becoming a doormat isn't what mercy means. It means the fortitude of will, the strength to carry on.

Raheim: We should have **loyalty** with respect to our views and our beliefs. All these are internal. It's very much like Shakespeare said: "To thine own self be true." The complexity of your unique-

§ 82 §

ness must be put forth. No one else has the right to push you in any direction against your will.

Each person probably has a different understanding of what **honor** means. Of all the keys, it's probably the most nebulous, because we don't always know what it means to be honorable. Most feel that it has to do with right actions. All of you should honor your physical self by nurturing and taking care of it. Sylvia is probably more of a stickler for honor than for any of the other keys. She has protocol, right actions, and right speech. Honor extends to treating other people honorably. Each person, as we know, is part of God. You honor the divine spark within them, regardless of their actions or appearance.

Which key is "living with our decisions"?

It's honor, absolutely. While you stand by the decisions you make, however, remember that other people's decisions are just as valid. Living your truth doesn't mean ramming it down the throats of others.

Gratitude seems to be almost an ambiguity. You don't need to be walking around being grateful to everyone and everything. That creates almost a false humility, which is disgusting. Have gratitude for being in this life, for learning. Only the strongest are allowed to come down.

Sylvia: If you live your life by the keys of gratitude and loyalty, you will never get derailed, you will never go off track, and you will never have any serious physical or mental or spiritual ills.

Loyalty takes in so much. It means, first of all, *loving yourself*—be loyal to yourself, loyal to your own virtues, loyal to your own feelings, and loyal to your own life theme. Most of all, be loyal to other people and to your religion and to your family and friends. This doesn't mean that we have to be loyal to people who are dishonest and awful or who don't care about us. That's stupid; that's loyalty misplaced. Once someone breaks loyalty with me, then our relationship is off. If they don't play fair, then they don't have to play at all.

The other one is **gratitude.** I think ingratitude, if there is such a thing as "sin," has got to be a "cardinal sin." We should be grateful for the fact that we can breathe, hear, and see. If we can't do any of those, like Helen Keller, you can touch. Ingratitude cripples the soul. Be grateful for just being here, experiencing for God. Positive people have happier lives.

Anytime you have a genuinely positive thought about someone, express it to them. Don't think they already know, or they will figure it out. I've seen movie stars and celebrities who don't date a lot, because everybody else thinks they wouldn't have a chance with them. They say, "I sit home every Saturday night alone" because no one thinks that they need anybody.

The other day a woman came in to deliver the mail to our office, and I hadn't seen her before. I was up at the front desk. I turned to her and said (and really meant it), "My, you're a beautiful woman." She was. She just glowed with beautiful white hair and big, blue eyes.

She later wrote me a card, saying, "You must have known this was a day in which I felt ugly, unloved, uncared for. Your words meant the world to me."

I will tell you right now what we women are sadly lacking in: We don't like to compliment men. That's a shame. Men are human beings, and they're very sensitive. Tell the man in your life that he is handsome and wonderful. Externalize what you feel and mean it. Stop being so closed up and icy. Give a loving hand. Let all your positive thoughts emanate from your soul.

Other Important Keys

Raheim: In actuality, there are countless keys that can further unlock your blossoming spirituality. Throughout, we have been drawing on the key of **love.** Another good example is **universal truth.** This key overlaps honor in that we must be true to ourselves.

To do that, we must recognize what our own inner truths are. Gnostic truth is very simple: It says that you will sustain yourself through life's experiences, you will learn, and then you will go Home. As a part of this, do a kindness every day, as Francine suggests. That's how you evolve. It's as simple as that.

Always remember that inner truths are individual and are all valid. Two people can disagree absolutely on an issue and both be right. Your God is different from another person's God, yet it all forms one amazing whole.

Pride has always been looked at as being a violent, negative thing, but pride in yourself must follow love of yourself, and in that sense it's a positive. Be proud of who you are inside, and carry yourself with pride and honor.

Seven Rays of God

Francine: The Seven Rays of God are not to be confused with any other theological premises that have been heretofore given, such as the levels of the soul or the tenets. This is separate and unique unto itself. It's very important for you to know these Seven Rays. In knowing these Seven Rays, or I should say, Seven Vibrations, you can go into these vibratory areas in your meditations by just asking to go.

Because the world is in such turmoil, by asking to go into these vibratory stages, you do an awful lot of *purification of your soul.*

The **first ray** is a direct emanation from God. It's known as a "thought ray," the first "beginning" of the created force. This vibration is probably the highest one, where the Thought of Creation began. When I say that, of course, you must know that I mean the plural—both Mother and Father God—is the Thought. We see it as a **silver** light vibration when we look at the Godhead, but the form cannot be held for any length of time.

God the Father can take a form, but very briefly—whereas Azna can hold Her form in constancy. This isn't because She is at a lower vibrational level, but because She rules the planets, so Her vibration is thicker. His vibration is more ethereal, so it's harder for the condensation to occur. The first ray is the emanation of both Godheads, both Mother and Father God. In the first vibration, the thought splits into male and female, which then continues *ad infinitum.*

Are the seven rays an energy force?

Absolutely: They are the motor, the vibratory energy of God. The rays are the evolution of God's thought, of which you're part. They show the sequence of God's thought processes. The **second ray** isn't as complicated; it's where thought condensed into matter. You're made of matter before you ever come down. You have many times a different visage, a different weight, a different coloring, and sometimes a different sex.

It's strange, because when we were first created, we all looked almost identically alike, almost like an archetype. Then we began to create our own image of what we liked. Or because our persona is different—themes and personalities began to hone our features. Some grow in beauty, and some grow in ugliness.

The second vibration is blue in color. It's very, very dark **blue**, sapphire blue. It's very hard to tell you what our colors are, because our colors are living colors. By this I mean that they actually breathe and vibrate.

Strangely enough, as these Rays spill out from the Godhead, they seem to diffuse. They're very dark closest to the center—to the "Heart of the Matter," as we say, to the Created Force. As they come forward, they lighten.

The **third ray** was the dispersing of entities, which means that everyone decided where they were going to go and how many lifetimes they would have. At this point, we chose our themes. Now, even though you have a certain theme for every life, there is always what we call the overall dharma responsibility that you're trying to perfect.

For instance, if your theme is basically Patience, then that would be your core; then, even though you might have picked Experiencer and Catalyst or any other thing, this would be the ultimate "over-soul" that you would carry with you. From the very "beginning," you took not only your theme, but also your ultimate oversoul. So you would be going through life after life learning Patience. The color is **green**, very emerald green.

The **fourth ray** is the evolution of the soul, to whatever level that soul wishes. This is where the record really starts now, showing the individual program that you chose, of what you're to perfect in this life. At this point, we were conscious of our plan, but we had yet to live it. You had the whole book, but you hadn't read it yet. Mother God helped us plan our lives because She rules the planets and knows its pitfalls. Many times I've seen Her sit and argue with people and Council about charts. She always wins. There is no winning against the Queen.

The color vibration here is **orange.** This is significant. Buddhists picked up the orange robes, didn't they? The setting sun, the orange robes. This is the evolution of the soul. The same as when you came in with your oversoul of Patience or Responsibility, so did you come in with God's Mind as to what you were going to evolve to. This is what we call "soul evolution."

Once we start living out our plan, there is some minor variation that's almost inevitable.

Raheim: The **fifth ray** is how much knowledge you gain from personal effort. You can pick your theme, you can be made flesh, you can evolve to a certain extent, but you have to seek knowledge. People stop; even the whitest of white entities will stop. Dark entities never seem to wear out. White entities have a tendency to wear out faster because they're not in their element on planet Earth. Most white entities don't understand that there is an individual part of God that protects them and gives them guardianship. That's truly the guardianship of the mind.

At this point—between the fourth and fifth ray—many quit searching, listening, and learning. By closing their mind off, they become senile and weakened, because there is no new information coming in. As Sylvia always says, "If you don't use it, you lose it." People are too ready to let someone think for them, and that's dangerous. That's how all cults begin.

Gnosis is all around you, and it's within you to seek it. Unfortunately, some negate knowledge, which is probably one of the worst ways that you can "miss the mark." Regardless of what path you take to gain knowledge, you must always be in the state of acquiring knowledge—s. Sometimes wrong knowledge, sometimes knowledge that isn't factual, but you're still gaining knowledge. We must sift through and separate the wheat from the chaff, as Jesus says.

Garner knowledge everywhere—pick it up, but make sure it fits you. Not everyone can follow the same pattern. That's where religion has been so wrong. What is very magnificent is that there is a true love of true knowledge. When you begin to ascend higher, then everyone's knowledge, strangely enough, begins to converge into an ultimate truth.

Universal Truths are very simplistic, devoid of avarice and greed. That means not hurting anyone. Very simplistic—doing good, but understanding that you're human. The one thing you fight constantly is the humanness of yourself. That was meant to be, though; you were meant to fight the flesh. Control your false ego—it is much more important to think of yourself as a puzzle piece that links everyone together. The fifth ray is colored **mauve.**

The **sixth ray** is experiencing knowledge, activating it in a physical setting. The rays become stronger as we proceed. The sixth ray is **white.**

Can anyone imagine what the final, **seventh ray** would be? You have now gone through the steps, so the seventh ray is the culmination of everything—going Home and staying. You go back at last—not into nebulous thought, but staying within glorified flesh, going back and making a total circle. Notice how seven keeps repeating itself. It's very powerful, as powerful as nine. The Bible and most mystical books often speak of seven. Any numbers divisible by three or seven are very mystical.

Does that mean going Home to Nuvo?

To Nuvo or to your original place; it means going back and getting the full mantle of Mystical Traveler. You may wonder if, from that point, you will start out again, and the Thought will again become flesh? No, although you may go to another planet if you choose after some time. I don't want to say centuries, because we don't know what that means. But sometime you might be called to other planets, but certainly not anything like this planet; nothing is like this one. But certainly you might be called on to travel to another place, whether in spirit form or in flesh. Mystical Travelers never seem to stop. That's the meaning of the name. They carry with them the mantle of salvation.

What color is the seventh ray?

It depends on which color you absorb; that's really more individualistic. It becomes your own aura. Then you can pick any color that you want. Most of you picked either gold or purple; some of you picked silver. It's really a matter of taste.

How can we strengthen our rays?

I would get all the colors involved in your aura. Name them all. For my own seventh ray, I love the silver. White you do automatically, anyway. Of course, you know the green is for illness or protection, but use them all. I don't like red very much. Use the shade of mauve instead. You have your aura banding around you, and then you have the rays of different colors that emanate from your seven chakras.

When we see you get up in the morning, your auras are too close to the body. This shows depletion of energy. When you go to bed tonight, I want you to say that when you get up tomorrow morning, your aura will extend two feet out from your body. Then it will be full and strong. You pull it in close because the darkness is so threatening, but I guarantee that if you get those rays going outward, people will come up to you and say, "Wow, you look brilliant. You look stunning, as if you have a light on inside of you."

🦋   🦋   🦋

Anything that you can ask, can be answered.
There are no mysteries.
— Sylvia

🦋   🦋   🦋

When knowledge is infused, usually suffering is taken away.
— Francine

🦋 🦋 🦋 🦋 🦋 🦋

§ Chapter Five §

LETTERS TO THE UNIVERSE

Raheim: Today I am going to ask you to buy something, a fresh, brand-new blank notebook. I don't want you to write down any of your problems in it; it won't be a diary. Rather, you will write letters to the Universe.

I'm going to show you, in one week's time, how powerful it becomes. Let's just start with a minor type of thing. I want you to consider whether you have an irritating or less-than-desirable boss or co-worker. It doesn't make any difference whether they're a dark entity. Let us negate their influence. In your notebook, write them a letter using their full name—first and last. Names are so important for identification. This gives you more power than just "To whom it may concern." I want you to pour out your heart and give all the points showing why you should *not* be treated the way you're being treated. Why you *do* need a raise. Plead your case specifically and clearly, with details about what you want changed.

You will be amazed—you can effect a Gnostic miracle. Let us say you have a legal case pending. Try to get the name of the judge and of the attorney for the opposing side; write them a letter posing your case. You can also write a letter to your child—or you and a friend can write letters for each other if, for example, one of you is having problems with a relationship. Write about how you should be treated, and what remedies should be effected. Plead your case in your name toward this person.

Never, ever send the letter. Keep it in your notebook. It doesn't ever have to be seen—just writing it is enough. It's effective. The more of you who write letters pleading a certain case, you will be amazed at the success rate. After you write your letters, read them out loud in front of a mirror to multiply your effectiveness. After that, illustrate the situation in your book. Employ every sense: You live in a world of tangibles, and you're constantly bombarded by textures, smells, and sounds. Your drawing can be mere stick figures, but put dialogue with them. After writing their discussion, have the two stick figures come together and embrace. You can even add scent and music. Pick out a particular song that makes your heart soar and that you won't tire of; then pick out a certain scent that will go along with this.

You don't have to do any ritualistic things, like burning your letters at midnight under a full moon. Just leave them in your book. If you're afraid that someone may read them, I think that you could destroy them; there is no problem with that. But I think it would be very nice to keep a book of letters.

You must write from the heart. Something like, "Please don't be so hateful to me. I wish you no harm. Try to let the real you come forward. If you do have darkness around you, please don't let it come over on me. Not just for myself, but for you, also." Be eloquent enough to get right to the mark.

You can express righteous anger or even be aggressive, as long as it's coming from the pure motive of wanting to effect a change. However, always temper such emotion with reason. You can use heart, but use reason, too. If you end up with a rambling letter full of nothing but anger, you might be very dismayed the first time you face the person you have written about. This person may be just as angry because this really hits the mark. So soft-peddle it with reason. You can get your righteous anger out, but make sure that it's reasonable and that you have the right intent. You can say in there, "I don't know why you dislike me; I'm not sure why I dislike you. I'm just pleading my case."

If it's a health issue, then you may not yet know a name to appeal to. Of course you can address God, but let me suggest that you write to your doctor or to any doctor or who may come into your life. Leave an open-ended name, and a blank that you can fill in later. You can write to the person who will come into your life, and say, "I command the Universe to send this person." When that person comes in, please have sense enough to fill in the blank. Similarly, if you have a legal problem, write to the Universe and ask that you be sent a great attorney.

Miracles are realities. In this, be selfish in a positive sense. There is nothing wrong with asking for something for yourself. Don't be afraid that you might limit the miracle if you list specific items to occur. The miracle, when it comes in, will not only take in what you have asked, but will give you more.

Let's say there is someone whom you're involved with who has caused you a great amount of pain, such as dealing with an addictive problem. You can elicit that addictive problem, and then elicit the fact that the person is well, happy, healthy, and strong. Then add that they're not cruel to their mother anymore, or cruel to their father, or cruel to you.

People tend to write about their past pain. You're going to write about what you're *becoming*. Put in your sense of tomorrow and the goals you wish to accomplish from this point on. Give your God-center to it. Make a covenant and a seal with the universe.

In addition, put a "due date" for your results.. I think you should time your situations. However, know that this isn't a one-shot thing. This is always ongoing.

Finally, write yourself a letter. Write what you aspire for yourself: what you wish, what you want, what you aspire to be. Write about the goodness of you. Don't write about your negatives: "I lied when I was four. I committed adultery when I was 40." The Universe doesn't care about that. Put it out of your mind. The greatest sin you have committed, if there is such a thing, is against yourself—it is the guilt you have carried. Say, "This is the first day of the rest of my life. I want to be more childlike, more giving, more caring."

MEDITATION—AT ONE WITH THE UNIVERSE

Put your hands upward on your thighs and call on all the Hosts of Heaven—God the Father, our dearest Mother Azna, and all the spiritual avatars who have lived to show others the way.

I want you to feel yourself sitting all alone, very quietly, cross-legged, hands upward in a very quiet, dark field at night. You're not afraid, because the darkness around you creates a protective mantle. You're sitting there in the darkness, and you're wishing for, and aspiring to, enlightenment. All of a sudden, in the far sky directly in sight of your third eye, there appears a tiny pinpoint of light; at first you think it might disappear with the blink of an eye. You sit transfixed by it.

As you focus on it, it becomes almost silvery blue. It becomes a little bit larger. Finally, you have to blink, and sure enough, it's still there. It opens larger yet. In an instantaneous emotion, a heartbeat second, this ray of silver-blue light shoots from the darkness, pierces through the night sky, and presses warmly into your very being.

All of a sudden, you're aware now that there are millions of tiny lights like fireflies beginning to dot the darkness. You feel bombarded in the most luxuriant way by all these pinpoints of light hitting different parts of your essence like a laser that cleans out darkness. All these fireflies of light now seem to be dancing around you.

Way off in the distance, you hear the sounds of the most unbelievable music, very soft at first, but beginning to roll stronger like a wave coming in. You can almost feel the molecules coming toward you. Every fiber in your being is now alert, and adrenaline is pumping life-giving fluid to every part of the body.

You know that you're synthesized with the universe—it is a part of you, and you're a part of it. All of a sudden, it's aware. Your uniqueness has addressed the universe. All the eyes and ears and feelings and emotion and beneficence is poured down now toward you. Over all that stands God— God the Mother, God the Father—watching, from a distance. What is even more miraculous is watching from the present, from the past, and from the future. The Caretaker.

You have now been given healing ability and the rapture. Splinters of light have been imbued in your body and can now shoot off your fingertips.

You stand in the field and shine like a silvery knight— armored, protected, sword glistening, smiling, fervent, loyal, honorable, dedicated, constant, responsible. Feel your foreverness, feel your continuation, feel your power. Ask this in the name of Our Lord to attend you this day for healing, comfort, and sanctity.

Bring yourself up, all the way up, feeling absolutely imbued with knowledge, inspiration, and healing.

Don't be so timebound. Concentrate on the wonders, rather than the suffering, of life. Change your routine from time to time. Be awake during different hours; eat at different times. You will have more energy and alertness. A small baby doesn't know the difference between day and night. They wake up, and they eat, and they do what they want. Monotony creates depression; it can even correlate to Alzheimer's.

Does exercise keep us younger?

Absolutely, you must exercise. You don't have to be jumping and running every single minute, but you've got to move your body. You have to walk and *do*. People think they have to always be in a gym. No, you've got to move and walk. The more you walk briskly and move around and bend, the body becomes lubricated. You stiffen without movement. It's like if you get too much sleep. I will tell you something. You think you feel bad from getting too little sleep. Get a lot of sleep, and see how you feel—like a groggy zombie. The more sleep you get, the more sleep you want. If you wake up in the middle of the night, do something. Don't be time-bound; in this way you will have more energy.

When you were younger, you ran and jumped and whirled; and it was fun. Do you remember when you were younger, how much fun it was to run?

MEDITATION—TIMELESS VACUUM OF PEACE

I want you to close your eyes, put your hands upward on your thighs, and take a very deep breath all the way from the solar plexus. Exhale all negativity. Surround yourself, as always, with the brilliant gold light of Mother Azna. Let us use Her as the Moderator today, the Protectorate. We can call in the archetypes, the God Consciousness, but today let us use Her as the ultimate source who helps us on this journey.

You're lying in a round room, on a round bed that's very soft. You're looking up to a glass ceiling, which is so clear that you are not even sure it's made of glass. You can see all the stars in a very dark sky. All of a sudden, the bed begins to rotate very gently; you're not afraid, and you don't have to hold on.

All of a sudden, you're surprised to be propelled up toward the ceiling, bed and all. For just a moment, you blink, ready for impact. But the skylight opens with a whoosh, and you're spiraling up in that dark sky, faster and faster, beyond speed, beyond light. For a moment, you take in breath, still aware that our Mother is with you watching and protecting. Faster and faster you go up into this night sky. The stars and planets whiz by.

You say to yourself, "How far will I go? To infinity? To eternity?" For just a moment, because you're in human form, you may feel that you're alone. Then all of a sudden, you realize that you're a total complete universe within yourself, with the beating heart of God, with the Mother watching out for you, with God encompassing the God Consciousness, with the Holy Spirit all around you.

All of a sudden, the bed drops away from you. For a moment you're without support, and for a moment, your arms stretch out. You feel like you might want to fight the air. Just when you feel that you might be afraid—a serenity envelops you. You suddenly realize that, not only can you breathe, but you're in a very quiet, peaceful vacuum. You look around, and there are stars. You can see for infinity.

The thing that strikes you the most is that you're with yourself in this quiet domain of timeless beauty taking stock of yourself, the emptiness of time and space. For whatever was back there, the seasons, the time, the days, the hours, the weeks, the months, are all irrelevant to you in this timeless vacuum. It's just you. The beating heart of you, the God-centered in you, and the God outside you.

Feel how insignificant all those times were. You're far enough away and removed that nothing is asked of you, nothing is expected. There are no responsibilities, no obligations. All of a sudden, little by little, like an onion that's peeled, the overlays of all the "have-to's" and "I-should-have-dones" are beginning to pull away. It's just you and the God in you in this timeless space. It's your refuge encased and floating, quiet, breathing, peace in the dark sky. All of a sudden, you're imbued with all the love and all the quiet peace that you will ever be able to get in an Earthly form. You're full of glory, you're full of awe, you're full of peace.

Now you're in free-fall, but you're not going so fast that you're frightened. You're observing as you go. What would happen if you got to Earth, and it was no longer there? Where would you land? For a moment there is a little bit of hesitation and maybe fear. Then you realize that you would be with yourself, with loved ones, and with God. Earth is only a figment of your imagination, but you do fall to Earth and through the skylight and to the bed. Each time you go out, create this vacuum of timelessness in space and time—the empty, quiet peace.

I guarantee that each time you go, upon awakening you will feel more rejuvenated than you ever have before, without any doubt. Bring yourself up to your consciousness feeling rested, quiet.

MEDITATION FROM FRANCINE— RELEASING CELL MEMORY

Relax your feet. I want you to put a very intense purple light around yourself; make it pulsate, and now begin to move with your purple light up your feet. I want you to say to your cell memory that you're right now releasing any negative cell memories that you have had in any part of your feet.

I want you to move up into the ankles and into the calves of your legs, and I want you to feel that it's releasing any bad cell memories there. While we're doing this, I want you to start "youthing" yourself. In other words, you're going to become younger and vital. The cells are going to stop their aging processes for a while, or slow it down. Of course, you're going to age, but you're going to do it at a slower pace. You're going to tell your cells that you're 20 years younger than you are.

Some of you are having knee problems. Concentrate very strongly on the knees, left and right knee. Any cell memory that has to do with past trauma, such as being cut off, tortured, or hurt in any way, the cell memory will readjust itself like a computer chip, and immediately begin to knit and heal the kneecap, behind the knee, and create its own vacuuming process—even torn ligaments, tendons that need to be tied up and tightened. Tell yourself that you will be flexible, not stubborn.

Moving up to the thighs, again tell the cell memory that any negativity is released. Move into the pelvic girdle and the reproductive system. Any cell memory that has caused any problem will immediately be released. Moving all the way up through the trunk of the body wherein all the organs reside, any cell memory, morphic resonance of past will be released.

This is a different body, a different time. Demand that the cells recover and begin to form their own positive memory adjustment. The same as the "I Am" adjustment. All of it is welded together—mind, body, spirit and the "I Am." Moving all the way up through the stomach into the digestive tract addressing the cell memory. Also telling the cell memory that you can gain or lose weight at will. Whatever morphic resonance of the cell memory that you may have starved—whatever may be the problem—let it be normalized.

Moving up through the whole chest area, into the lungs, the vascular system, the heart area, the upper lung and bronchial area, and all the organs therein—any cell memory that's causing any problems from now until the end of your life will be released. Not only have we moved into the digestive area, but let us move around to the back and to the sides of not only the pancreatic area, but the liver, the kidneys. Let us move right up the whole endocrine gland system.

Any traumas we have taken into our cell memory of our body, let it be released. Into the bladder area, into the lymphatic area, let the cell structure of the lymphatic area come up, because the lymphatic area is really the controlling of infection. Bring the lymphatic system up very high, and bring your temperature up one degree for just a few minutes. You may be surprised that you immediately start heating up.

Why I want you to demand that your cellular structure bring your temperature up to one degree, is you know perfectly well that the temperature gauge is what burns out any illness.

It's not there to make you sick. It's there to burn out. It's a heating unit—a very, very complex and miraculous heating unit. So bring your temperature up one degree. You will find that you are getting very warm: Your hands are getting warm, your face is getting warm, the warmth is spreading all over you. Now readjust your temperature down. When you feel that you're getting any infection, demand that your temperature rise, that your lymphatic system kicks in to high gear, that your spleen also kicks into high gear. You're not going to destroy your body by doing that. If you need to have more energy, don't be afraid to address the cell structure of the adrenal area. You're not going to wear your adrenals out.

From the very top of your head now, even into your eyes, your nose, your throat, and especially the mind, the physiological mind—ask that it immediately gets rid of its own ego-structure and its holding on to the humanity of yourself and giving over control to the higher mind or the superconscious to the immediate control center. You will immediately be above the body, which will then allow your body to be in its own perfect immune state without letting the mental thoughts get into the physiological body.

Also demand that you're unprogrammable. You won't listen to any negative programming coming from anyone that will talk you into illness. You won't let them feed you into this. You will be the champion, the monitor, and the chief person in your personage of yourself. That's the controller of

*your own ship. That's what the Gnostics believe. That's what
they have always believed, that you're the captain of your
own ship.*

*Feel the quiet peace in your cell memory begin to quiet
and become clean, eased, efficient, healed, in perfect accord.
You have learned from it; you don't need to keep enduring
it. Please do this for a week. After you do so, you're going to
be quite amazed at how absolutely your body begins to adjust
to this cell memory. Bring yourself out to your complete
consciousness.*

Keep Your Power

Francine: There is a universal pattern that you have to watch
out for: "I have power, but then I give my power away. Then I
take my power back, and then I give it away." This seems to be a
universal human characteristic. Say: "I will empower myself with
my will and my judgment."

This pattern happens more between a male and female than it
does between two males or two females. Females have a tendency
to give their power away too easily. You all know the societal, religious, and historical reasons behind this. Patriarchy hasn't been balanced by the feminine principle.

You all probably had parents or people around you who have
lived lives of Victim and Victimizers. This is probably one of the
most common karmic patterns. It need not be that women are total
emotion and men are total intellect and control. No one should give
away half of themselves. A pair of people can get unbalanced in
this way even if both are the same sex.

The roles should be, "I'm an entity unto myself, and you're an
entity unto yourself. I respect the God-center within you, and you
must respect mine." Get the total compensation of your own self-
esteem. That doesn't mean you're power-crazy. It means you're
empowered with your "I Am," which is that unique part of God

that you must protect.

You may become at a certain point more assertive, which you all should be, male and female both, especially if you think you're in the right. Some will say, "But how do I know if I'm right?" You have every right to be heard, including your religious view. Gnosticism is very open and welcoming; any path to know God is valid, if it is based upon love.

Gnostics are tolerant, which means, "I respect your views and I allow you to have them, but I'm not going to bow to them if I don't believe them." The main person you have to honor and respect is yourself. Monitor your patterns. Respect the God within.

Consider the example of Jesus' life. He preached love, goodness toward others, and respect for everyone. But he was against the judgment of the Sanhedrin, the Jewish court system. In church, he called them Pharisees, which in that time meant "bloodsucker." He said, "You preach nothing but greed and the fear of total damnation." He wanted no part of it.

Stand up tall. Let your inner God guide your actions. *Self-esteem,* in contrast to *ego,* means: "I'm proud of myself for what I've done and what I know I can do." Ego really has no experience or knowledge. Self-esteem is *knowing* you can do something. That's judgment and will and knowledge.

Mirroring

Raheim: I'm going to show you how to facilitate a method called "mirroring." It's a very high-powered method of channeling. First I'm going to explain it to you, and then I'm going to help you do it in meditation. First of all, construct a very large mirror in your mind. Think about the reflection of self.

MEDITATION—THE MIRROR

Put your hands upward on your thighs in a meditative position and relax yourself. I always like putting your energy into your third eye. A very strong way to do that is to think of yourself surrounded, of course, with the White Light of the Holy Spirit. We have the God Consciousness around you. We have the Mother and Father God and all the archetypes and archangels around you.

I want you to visualize a dark velvet sky. When you do, begin to see one singular star in it, coming closer and closer to you and becoming brighter and brighter, almost blue-white with silvery edges. As it comes closer, it literally goes right into your forehead. No pain, but when it does, you almost feel as if something has been opened. It almost sparks in you a feeling of opening and release right in the pituitary gland area, which does look like a small eye.

Keeping this star right in the middle of your forehead, I want you to face a very ornate, full-length mirror with gold scrolling around it. You're standing in front of this mirror, and you're seeing yourself. I want you to take yourself, in a relaxed state, back and back and back. Before you ask for a certain person to come up in front of you in this state, ask for anyone that your mind needs to address to show themselves in that mirror.

Don't, under any circumstances, wave anyone away, even if they're not familiar to you. This may be someone from a past life or even a parental figure or a grandparent that maybe you have never met. Whoever this person is that stands in front of you, ask them to speak and verbalize any message to you. You might even have a Master Teacher show up, even your guide. At first the image may seem fuzzy, because you have taken up the space of the mirror. But then all of a sudden, superimposed upon your countenance and your form, reflected is this other person. Receive your message now.

Now, I want you to pick out from your consciousness a particular figure. First I want you to pick out a person who maybe you never got resolution with, maybe you never got to say what you wanted to say to, living or dead. Bring that person up as you did before, standing in front of you. Maybe it's a lover who left you and hurt you; maybe it's a family member you could never, ever, make an inroad to; maybe it's someone who has passed over that you couldn't ever forgive. This is a time to be able to speak your mind and plead your case. See what they say back. If they don't say anything back, it's fine. There is something truly magic, I say this in the most holiest of words, that has to do with the mirrored image of someone who has harmed you or hurt you, in which you can ventilate and not harm them, but expunge yourself from the wrath or the abuse or the hurt.

Now reflect someone whom you love dearly. Perhaps you never got a chance to say good-bye to them, or to finish off whatever you needed to. Or maybe they're still living with you and you would like to say a lot of things that you can't say to their face. In doing this, you're going to find out that you're mirroring their soul. This is the one way you can get them to "get it." It's even more powerful than writing letters to the Universe. See if they can speak back.

Now pick out someone who right at this moment in time you're having a terrible problem with—whether it's a co-worker, a spouse, a child, or even a friend. I want you to put that person in front of you and plead your case through rational discourse. Keep emotion, if you can, out of it. Preferably use someone whom you can't seem to change, or seems uncontrollable in their lifestyle. Someone who you feel hates you at work that has been a block to you. As much as you may detest this person, I want you to mirror your love and your petitioning toward them.

In no way, shape, or form are you telepathically, or any other way, trying to control or manipulate or brainwash or use any other occult practices. It's a type of what we call "imitative magic." Sending love all the time, but you can still have enough righteous anger to plead your case.

Now open your mirror out. You didn't realize that it's hinged. I want you to line these people up mentally. You now see the person that hurt you in childhood, the person you absorbed who you wanted to be like, the person who was a block, the person maybe who is passed who you never got resolution with. You can fill up as many mirrors as you want. Now have them all reflected toward you. You send them love and demand that they give forgiveness and love and self-esteem and respect back and forth. If there was a loved one you didn't get a chance to say good-bye to, have them come in to the mirror and give you a message. You might be surprised that certain people show up that you never expected, living and dead. Wish them well, wish them God's speed, God's blessing.

Pull yourself back to yourself, keeping the brilliant star in your forehead. Don't lose that star. If you want to increase your own psychic insight and healing ability, keep that star. That's your own personal star. Bring yourself back to yourself in a wide-awake position.

In conjunction with the letter-writing, let's say you have a court trial or something that's very hard to go through, or an interview with a difficult person. Before you do it, visualize that person in your mirror, speak to them, and get a message. I'm telling you, there is nothing more miracle-bearing than this. Let's say there's someone in your life who could be very addictive or has a lot of problems. If you keep this mirror going for a matter of three or four nights and you keep talking to that person in mirror image, I guarantee you that you're going to be in the thoughts of that person. That person is going to be invaded by your love and your empathy and sympathy.

෧   ෧   ෧

We really should call this a Psychic Mirror. It really begins to mirror an awful lot of psychic infusion. Perhaps you saw someone you were angry with, and something transcended the hurt. You became more gracious in this transcendence. When you transform, you get a little bit above the earth realm. As you do, you get a little chunk of what we're about on my Side. That little piece, that golden piece, you bring down with you. Each time you bring it, the anger, the self-righteousness, the injustices begin to fade. They all become just so much old news. You can create a miracle.

In giving love out, light went into the mirror and came back into my third eye.

You can't send that much love out and not get it reflected back. Never wish any bad. Just petition your case again, send them love, and give them your justice, your truth. You will be surprised at how it neutralizes negativity.

Even if they don't even know it on a conscious level, you're asking for their soul to attend you. This is what some call "dream time," where the Aborigines used to go and visit, and what the Native Americans used to call the "sleep walkers." Their shamans said that their soul traveled at night and would go visiting.

In my time, when I used to teach my students, I would say, "This is the best way to transcend, and bring the other soul up to transcend with you."

෧   ෧   ෧

The only reason that you ever come together is to share a common knowledge that you're all working in a different area for God. Rather than saying you're of one mind, no, you're of one God with many minds.
— Raheim

*As you travel through your life, all the people whom you
have loved begin to gather around. The more spiritually
advanced you become, the more the crowd grows.*
— Francine

Chapter Six

SPIRITUAL PHILOSOPHY

Sylvia: The hardest thing that we ever have to learn, even though Jesus said it 2,000 years ago, is to love your neighbor as yourself. Most of us don't have a problem loving other people; the problem we have is loving ourselves. We always equate that with selfishness.

It has nothing to do with selfishness. It means having internal awareness that your God-center is linked up to God. You picked this life to come in to, and you have a theme to perfect, for God.

One of the tenets of our religion is: "The way of all peace is to scale the mountain of self. The love of others makes the climb down easier. We see all things darkly until love lights the lamp of the soul." (A list of all the tenets can be found later in this chapter.)

The Gnostic Christianity embodied by my church, the Society of Novus Spiritus, is very different from any other denomination of Christianity. As some of you might know, I'm a student of religions. I have been in many of them and have studied most of them; I'm from a Jewish, Catholic, Episcopalian, and Lutheran background.

Listening to priests, ministers, rabbis, and others, I always got the feeling that they "knew," and we didn't. They made us feel stupid. Through all of my studies, I began to realize that all of the messiahs said that if we were like children, we would understand it.

The movement that everybody calls "the New Age" isn't new. It's older than time. It was around long before the time of Buddha or the time of Jesus, and it came about way before the Old Testament. The whole world believed in it, totally and completely— we have had many lives.

We're Gnostics—not agnostics. I want this to be a people's religion. We base our path to God on reason far more than on faith. Anything that you can ask can be answered. There are no mysteries. A truth and a reality that you never believed possible will manifest inside you. Believing on faith alone is exhausting. *Reason* is what we're bringing you. The whole idea is that God is in His heaven, and you're here. The reasonable idea is that you keep progressing, that whatever wrongdoings have been done to you, they are ultimately for a reason. Nothing is random or pointless.

This is the first time in 2,000 years that we're merging a belief in reincarnation into Christianity. For years and years, people didn't believe these two ideas went hand in hand, but of course they do. Scholars and theologians tell us that the Gnostics and the Essenes had extensive writings about reincarnation up until A.D. 325 with the Council of Nicaea. So did our Lord, because he studied in India.

I'm going to give you techniques so you can live more fully with your own religious beliefs. What you have to realize is that Gnosticism doesn't care whether you're Lutheran, Catholic, Jewish, Protestant, or Buddhist. We are an addition to your existing beliefs, not a replacement for them. The main issues in founding my church are:

- to love, not fear, God
- to get rid of guilt; and
- to show that through many lifetimes you perfect your soul, then return to the Other Side.

This knowledge also helps you progress faster and not have to come back so many times. If you want to, that's fine. But I'm sure most everyone is weary of it, or they wouldn't be searching. We're tired of the guilt, of the fear, and of laboring through life.

This doesn't mean that life can't be wonderful, but it's hard. This religion means that we're going to join hands, and make it from one shore to the other with all of us interconnecting, so you will always have a place to go and a back-up support system.

The reason, I think, that most religions have failed is that there has been so much fear and guilt, so much emphasis on hell and the devil. That's the biggest joke in the world. *This* is hell. You don't have to worry about devils. We have enough nasty, mean people running around. If you don't believe me, drive in rush-hour traffic.

The only time you should feel guilty is if you do something maliciously and with premeditation—but how many of us do that? Do you feel guilty because you don't love your parents, or you don't care about them as much as you should? Maybe they're unlovable. Do you feel guilty because you don't feel that you're a good enough parent? Maybe you have lousy kids. Did that ever dawn on you? It has on me. That doesn't mean that you dump them somewhere, but understanding and tolerance gets better.

Don't get caught up in, "I should do, I have to do, I had better do," as do many of my clients. Nobody gives us a manual on how to live this life. We write our chart, but no one gives us pamphlets or says, "Look, this is what it means to be a good spouse, a good worker, a good friend, a good parent, or whatever."

Let's face it—we all chose to come down. We even chose all of our family members, and they chose us. If there is no negativity in life, then you don't perfect for God. Now, I know what some of you are thinking: *What was wrong with me when I picked these challenges?* On the Other Side, as I've said so many times, everything is so wonderful and magnificent that we say, "Hey, I will handle that," because we're so happy and close to God. Then we get down here, in this vehicle we call the body, and it gets really tough.

One message I want you to hear clearly is: *Don't have a fear of God.* Why should you be afraid of the Supreme Being from Whom you came? Wouldn't it be terrible if our children, every time they came in the room, crawled in on their hands and knees in a sup-plicating position? That isn't love. Love means standing proud: "I'm your child. I'm standing here with my head held high, feeling proud that you created me."

How could something that God created be putrid and unwor-thy? What are you unworthy of? Wouldn't you feel terrible if some-body said to you that your genetics stink? Of course, and that's really what we're saying by groveling around—we're saying to God that His creations are not good.

If we've lived many lives, we're going to go through everything, but we have got to be able to hold each other's hands along the way. We've got to be able to say, "I'm here with you."

There is nothing you're going to escape. Everyone goes through trauma in life, because God is an "Equal Opportunity Employer." He doesn't give you just one chance to be a mess—He gives you lots of chances, until finally the pattern stops. We keep going on until we get it right. The minute you realize what your pattern is, you can begin to release it from you.

But there is hope, there is joy, and there is love. We've got to be a beacon of light to others. Many of you who have been with me for years know my dream of the last 20 years: I want a tem-ple, I want a hospice, I want an old people's home, I want a place for animals, I want a children's school, and I want a place where everyone can go regardless of faith or denomination.

Too many people think that we need huge cathedrals with crys-tal domes. I don't think so. We will meet in fields, or we will meet under the stars, in nature, holistically. Like I've said so many times to my people, don't come if you expect a big building. Come because you want to say to someone, "Are you searching?" And the other person says, "Yes, I'm intellectually searching, and I must find the answer."

You don't have to come to any one place, unless you want reinforcement. You don't need a lot of ritual or ceremony. We don't have to go to a church, because our spirituality is *inside* us, but every once in a while, we need to reach out and ask: "Do you feel like me? Do you think like me?" It's wonderful to grasp a hand and hear the answer, "I do." Then you don't feel so alone, so crazy, so ill.

I want you to have something to take with you that lasts you throughout the week. I want you to have a living, breathing religion. Before, it was "fear God and don't sin." The *only* sin that you can ever commit is against yourself—by not loving yourself enough. If you don't love yourself, you can't love or care about anybody else, and you won't.

Live your life with joy; allow yourself to be. Give yourself that sanction.

Loving yourself also means getting over yourself. Stop with this, "Me, me, me—I deserve." Don't be dependent; be strong. The spirit of God moves in every one of us; the spark of God ignites. Is it a big formula? No, all you have to do is ask for it and accept it. That's really your baptism.

When I say that we have each written our chart, people say, "Well, that's so predestinationist." No, it isn't. Don't you realize that it's a security? Think about it rationally. No matter if you're the biggest mess in the world, you can't fail.

People ask, "Am I off track?" Yes, they can be, because the charts have a certain amount of freedom within them. Of course, it's when we veer off too far that illness starts. But the basic course of getting from one shore to the other is fixed; you better believe you're going to make it—via spirituality and knowing that God is within you.

We're afraid to die, we're afraid to live, and in between, we're a mess. We have illnesses, we have anxieties, and we feel lost and useless a lot of the time. We don't like getting older, and we don't like being young. When we're young, we don't know what we're doing. When we're older, we feel that nobody is going to listen to us anyway. We don't know if we're on track, what good we have done in our life, if our life means anything, and what our purpose is.

The hardest thing you ever do is "climb the mountain of self."

We've been programmed to serve our self, not only from this life, but from all of our other lives, from the overlays, the behaviors, and the phobias that we carry—when in truth, your job is to get over yourself.

If you have a phobia, when you go to bed at night, surround yourself with white light and say, "Whatever phobia I'm carrying from any life—of closed-in places, snakes, heights—let it be released in the white light around me." You will either lose it completely or make it nearly insignificant.

Don't waste your time with people who enjoy their pain. Don't waste your time with martyrs. People say, "Well, isn't it my karma to suffer?" No. If you're aggravated about it, then that's a good sign, isn't it? Something is rising in your soul that means you're tired of it. It's your karma to act on that, separate yourself from it, and be done with it.

Trust yourself. God's finger does move inside you.

People use the word *karma* now, where they used to use *hell*: "It's my karma to live with this jerk who beats me up." What karma, that you're masochistic? If you stay on longer with something, like a job, or a relationship that irritates and really, really aggravates you, then you're not doing anything but upsetting your nervous system and creating an illness.

Loving unconditionally is the hardest thing to accomplish. To say, "I love the fact that you just exist in this world, that you passed my way, and that I could love you," is enough.

Can't we just get to the point that we're collectively loving, holding hands, and being in love? We Americans can't touch each other, can we? We're scared. Europeans think we're crazy. And such isolation can indeed make us nuts: Our nerve endings and the whole surface of our body get crazy. It really affects us; we become an island.

We're afraid of our emotions. Yet shying away from them is what causes illness. Why did God put anger and pride and everything else within us? Do we think it's because the flesh is supposed to be weak?

Flesh isn't weak. To this day, doctors don't know exactly how the heart beats. The physiological system is the most magnificent machine in the world. Can any other mechanism go on working for over 100 years?

Be joyous. Be happy. Be imbued with the true Christian spirit that God is love.

Don't be afraid to ask someone to hug you, or to oblige if you're asked. If you really want to know, psychically, what a person is truly like, you just touch them. Have you ever done that? You think somebody is a certain way, then you touch them, and then you know much more. Learn to do that. *Psychic* means no more than your power from God to discern truth. Everyone can have it. It's marvelously empowering; I believe that we can all become empowered in this way.

Depend on yourself first. Then reach out for others who can reinforce you. See the beauty of the soul in you, and find those who allow it to flourish.

Realize that you are an indigenous, individual, unique spark of God and that the God Consciousness is moving inside you. Say, "I'm a channel for the Divine." We're all God. Every one of us collectively makes up the emotional side of God. When we go to the Other Side, there is no one who judges us but *us.*

Living a "spiritual life" means this: "I'm going to do as much good as I possibly can and live the best life I can. I'm going to give as much love and healing, and bless as many people, as I can. Then I'm going to graduate and go Home." It's as simple as that. We can be religious without having dogma. The minute we start imposing rules, we get critical and judgmental of others.

No one is harder on us than we are; no gigantic entity sits on a throne and says thunderously, "Look at you, just a rotten, lousy . . ."

I also feel that this is important: *You must have righteous anger.* Don't be wimpy or let people abuse you or hurt your feelings without a fight. They don't have the right to do that to you—to push you around, be mean to you, be hateful to you. That isn't compatible with the dignity of the God-self inside you.

I'm not suggesting that we should all have hatred and be mean and nasty. No, because that doesn't get us anywhere. But if somebody hurts us terribly, we need not allow it to continue. This is when you remove yourself from the situation.

You can stop the pattern of abuse in your life. You can stop being afraid and in the dark and alone. There is never a time when God isn't with you. Most people who are drawn to this message—I don't care whether you believe this or not—are on their last life, or want to finish up really fast. Francine says, "Anybody who embraces this philosophy wants to complete their perfection, go to the Other Side, and not return."

The Other Side

What is the Other Side like? It's a wonderful place in a dimension right on top of this one with religious centers, libraries, music halls, art centers, and everything that we have here—*except* the erosion and pollution and negativity. As Francine says, even if we lived 80 or 90 years, it's like a drop in the bucket compared to eternity. This doesn't mean life isn't precious, but why do you take yourself so seriously? Don't get caught up in an ego trip of how bad you are, or how silly you looked, or if you did this or that right. Throw the dice, for God's sake, and live life the best you can.

Our entire world is reproduced on the Other Side. Nothing that God makes is ever lost. People ask me, "Are my animals over there?" Of course they are. You think that God would negate what you love? Or that anything that was loved by you would never come back? What kind of unmerciful God is that? My guide said that when I go to the Other Side, I have so many animals to meet me that people can't get through. Well, haven't you ever had animals that were much more caring and loving and forgiving and understanding and loyal than any person could ever be?

My grandmother used to tell me to be wary of people who hate music, animals, and children.

MEDITATION—THE PURPLE FLAME

Put your hands upward on your thighs. I want you to relax yourself mentally, and start breathing in and out very regularly, simulating the rhythm of how you breathe when you sleep. Feel yourself becoming very relaxed. All the negativity is being released, almost like a spiritual baptism emanating throughout every single part of your body to create healing and burn out guilt, negativity, and fear. You're now healed in mind, body, and spirit.

Let this surge of relaxation go right through the very bottoms of your feet, cleansing out any illness through the calves, knees, thighs, buttocks, and spinal column. Up through the whole trunk of the body, down through the shoulders, the upper arms, the lower arms, the hands, the fingertips. Up through the neck, the face, and behind the eyes. Demand that all the negativity—anything that you have brought over from past lives that's causing phobias and illnesses—be rinsed clean. From this moment on, I guarantee that you're going to notice a difference. Spirituality is probably the most beautiful euphoria you will ever know. While you're sitting in this relaxed position, ask for a bubble of light to surround you. Just visualize or ask for it.

Now, a purple flame engulfs you, almost like a lotus blossom. Put yourself in its middle. The color purple is the greatest emanation of spirituality. Once our mind and spirit are together, our body follows suit. Feel this purple flame rinsing out any past-life overlays, any of the negativity we have carried with us, any of the hurts, the vengeance—feeling left out, unwanted, persecuted, victimized, laboring through, lonely, isolated. Feel it vibrating, emanating, cleansing out sickness in mind, body, and spirit.

Say to yourself, "My spirit can never be sick. What I'm carrying around as an overlay may be sick and heavy, but I'm going to drop that right now with the power of the Holy

Spirit and the God Consciousness."

Feel energy coursing up through the very bottoms of your feet, up through your ankles, your calves, your knees, your thighs. All through the trunk of your body, curing and healing every organ therein. Down through the shoulders, the upper arms, the lower arms, the hands, the fingertips. Up through the throat area (back and front), the face, around the mouth, the nose, the eyes. Demand again that the last vestiges of any illness or phobic-causing, fear-causing overlays will be released right now through the power of the Holy Spirit.

Bring yourself back to yourself by counting to three.

There is no chance, from this moment on, that you won't get better, that you won't feel more dignity of self, that you won't love yourself more. Don't be so concerned about who loves you, but be concerned about whom you love. Everyone wants to be loved, but the only way you're ever going to be loved is if you love unconditionally. That's what our Lord said. We made so many rules and regulations that we didn't know where it was anymore. Be able to turn to each other and say that you love each other.

Following are the Tenets of Novus Spiritus, which will help you in your quest to love each other more.

TENETS OF NOVUS SPIRITUS

I   The way of all peace is to scale the mountain of self. Loving others makes the climb down easier. We see all things darkly until love lights the lamp of the soul.

II   Whatever thou lovest, lovest thou.

III   Don't give unto God any human pettiness such as vengeance, wrath, or hate. Negativity is man's alone.

IV   Create your own heaven, not a hell. You're a Creator made from God.

V   Turn thy power outward, not inward, for therein shines the Light and the Way.

VI   In faith be like the wind chimes. Hold steady until faith, like the wind, moves you to joy.

VII   Know that each life is a path winding toward perfection. It's the step after step that's hard, not the whole of the journey.

VIII   Be simple; allow no man to judge you, not even yourself, for you can't judge God.

IX   You're a Light in a lonely, dark desert that enlightens many.

X   Let no one convince you that you're less than a god. Don't let fear imprison your spiritual growth.

XI   Don't allow the unfounded belief in demons to block your communion with God.

XII   The body is a living temple unto God, wherein we worship the spark of the Divine.

XIII   God doesn't create the adversities in life. By your own choice, they exist to aid in your perfection.

XIV   Karma is nothing more than honing the wheel of evolvement. It's not retribution, but merely a balancing of experiences.

XV   God allows each person the opportunity for perfection, whether you need one life or a hundred lives to reach your level of perfection.

XVI   Devote your life, your soul, your very existence, to the service of God, for only there will you find meaning in life.

XVII   War is profane; defense is compulsory.

XVIII   Death is the act of returning Home, it should be done with grace and dignity. You may preserve that dignity by refusing prolonged use of artificial life-support systems. Let God's will be done.

Considering Spirituality

The more you consider my Gnostic theology, the more you go back to the time of primitive humanity. Stop and consider that we have always had a need to worship the sun, or totems, or even the beetle that rolls a dung ball along the ground. We've always needed to believe in something beyond ourselves.

What about the feminine principle of God? People don't like to talk about that, because they think it sounds like witchcraft and all that. Of course it isn't—but what about us women? If we were made in the image and likeness of God, who made us? I do not accept that we came out of a rib. Most of us are too heavy. A little skinny rib with a head on it? I don't think so. Besides, read Genesis 1:26 very carefully, and you will see that God is plural in saying, "Let Us make man in Our image, according to Our likeness."

During our upbringing, we heard this, but we let it slide. But somewhere, our God-Consciousness, the Holy Spirit, kept whispering that the truth was being hidden from us.

Jesus wasn't the only great teacher; Buddha, Mohammed, and many more all say the same thing. They all try to tell us that God is good, loving, caring, and omnipotent. So from the earliest times, there has always been something higher; we need to feel this. Don't ever let anybody tell you they're an atheist. There is no such thing. Everyone worships something, even if it's only money.

Even to this day, in this age of knowledge, there are superstitious people. I had a woman come to see me sometime ago. She was sitting across from me as I was doing the reading. Like I said a million times, psychics are not smart when it comes to themselves. While I'm doing the reading, she was slowly unbuttoning her blouse.

I'm thinking, *Oh my God, I've seen everything now. I've got a flasher.* As I got through with my opening spiel—"I will tell you everything, and I'm not going to control your life. That's between you and God"—she threw open her blouse, shouting, "There!" and a giant crucifix is hanging around her neck.

I had to laugh. We have to make fun of life's tragedies. Did you know that? People who are hurt and upset, you've got to make them laugh. Laughter gets rid of all the negativity in your body . . . it does. Studies have found out that people who laugh a lot get well faster. They're doing this with cancer, too.

This religion won't save your soul, but it will make your soul worth saving.

You see, people such as the woman with the giant crucifix still think "psychic" is different from "spiritual." It's not. *The more psychic you become, the more aware you become.* The more aware you become, the more spiritual you become.

The Ancients knew this, that *psychic* meant "the power of the mind to discern truth." Jesus was the greatest psychic in recorded history. He had the power to discern what illness a person was suffering from. He knew exactly what to do for the people. The miracle was that he was psychic enough to let God's knowledge flow through him freely.

Every single one of us can have the Father guiding us. But you see, if you do what our Lord attempted, to make temples within every single person and to replace dogma with spirituality, that disrupts the establishment. No longer will the people pay someone else to be their religious leader. We're just going to say, "God, I'm here for You, to experience for You. I love You, and I know You love me," and be on our way.

"God is going to be mad at me," I hear people say. "I've already asked God for three things this week, so I can't ask Him for any more." Wrong. All through history, because of ignorance, the whole idea was to make God humanized for the common masses. In other words, if I put God in pants and a shirt, with a wart on His finger, then He becomes like us. But they made Him worse than us. They also gave Him every negative humanized emotion that we have, and He *cannot* have those. If God gets mean, nasty, hateful, cranky, and rotten, we have lost God, because then He isn't perfect, don't you see? People experiencing those feelings are the emotional side of God.

We've become neurotic because we're so afraid that God isn't going to forgive us. Forgive *us? We've got to forgive ourselves!*

As I relate this next item, you might say, "Oh, God, Sylvia, you have become blasphemous."

The Old Testament is a collection of teaching stories, but certainly not the word of God. The Bible is a wondrous book—but it's a storybook. Please know that it can be a very dangerous book as well, because people will use it to judge and condemn you. They take excerpts from it—not the full passage—then hammer you with it and make you suffer. I call these people "judgmentalists," because they do not follow Jesus' teachings at all.

What some of these people will often say is: "Deuteronomy said, 'Don't consort with seers and sorceresses.'" Who is a seer or a sorceress? I don't know anybody that is. What's more, the entire Bible is filled with prophecy. What about the first book of Samuel, in which Saul actually goes to a woman with the "divining spirit" who goes into trance to communicate with Samuel, who had been dead many years? Samuel himself was a "seer"; Saul consulted with Nathan, a "prophet."

Some argue, "No, that's only if God appoints them." What? Do we assume that the supply of messengers dried up after Jesus? Francine explained that the passage from Deuteronomy applied to a situation very much like ours. People who were literate Gnostics were trying to warn others against charlatans.

Every religion is based on a psychic with a prophetic insight. The only difference in my church, Novus Spiritus, is that everyone becomes more psychic; and it's all hands reaching to God, not just one central figure. I'm just one figure who said it's possible that you can be psychic. You see, the reason that established churches fear us is that we erode their power base and their money. We know that our salvation lies inside of us. The bigger we grow, the more power we have individually, as well as collectively—and the less we need a big cathedral with its endless need for money.

You see, we Gnostics are truer Christians than the judgmentalists, because we follow the words of Jesus—we believe in what he preached and taught. Go back to his original words. Where was his philosophy coming from? Of course from God, but he also studied throughout Asia during his "lost" years.

We want to be Gnostics like Jesus was. We want to do what he said, rather than follow the dogma created by man. We know for a fact through research and church history that there were about 15 books deleted from the Bible that had to do with reincarnation and Mother God. Research it yourself. Start with the Council of Nicaea, in the year A.D. 325.

Some people will ask, "You belong to a *psychic* church?" They don't understand that *psychic* and *spiritual* are synonymous. *Psychic* means "the ability of the mind to discern truth."

That's the definition. If we have to separate *psychic* from *religion,* then the entire Bible goes away. If you remove prophecy from the Bible, you've ruled out the first five scrolls, the first books of the Old Testament. If you rule out miracles and paranormal happenings, you rule out the gospels of Jesus. So you don't have much left except the later writings of people who did not even know Jesus.

It's not hard to be like Jesus. Go out and say, "Please love God. Be forgiving. Be kind. Don't be so condemning." Don't you find it so sad that people who say they're "Christian" judge everybody? Why is that? They're the first to throw stones. They say, "If you don't believe the way I do, you're going to go to hell." Did Jesus ever say that? No.

Ignorance is a dangerous thing. "I'm the only way" is never true. Highly advanced, spiritual people never think that. They keep truth within their heart, and they live it every day of their life, like Jesus did, like all the avatars and messiahs did.

How can we make these judgmental people feel better about themselves? What you can do more than anything is live as an example. You're not going to convince anybody of something. Your message will get around. Not by prancing up and down with labels and banners flying, but because you approach things with knowledge and intellect.

It's a tragedy. People who are not spiritually evolved cannot understand a concept based on love. This isn't being judgmental, because we were all there once, too. They only understand through fear, and that's their childlike evolution. Do you know how, as a small child, that sometimes you don't understand "hot"? So what must your parents do? Slap your hand a little bit the second time you touch the stove. That's who the judgmentalists are. They will get there someday, but how much does an eighth-grade student have to say to a kindergartner? Not much.

It's very, very responsible to believe the way we do. It's very evolving, and it's very spiritual. All of a sudden the Light shines, and we know.

Let the innate beauty of your soul provide a beacon of Light for others in this world of Darkness. Show others how to live; be an example for them. Choose joy, show a zest for life, love others, and make your own heaven. Light your lamp for them all to see. You will find it can smooth your path and hasten perfection.

Psychic Ability

People often ask me how they can become more psychic. I tell them, "You don't just learn it."

What happens is that your psychic ability begins to open up when it's used and when you're with other people who augment its development. Sometimes people in classes have had their psychic ability come up because of the energy in the room. It's something everybody was born with, and something everyone has.

You know who stops this? Religion, culture, society, and many "nice" parents stop it. As children, you had all kinds of psychic feelings about things, but when you asked your mother, she said, "No, I didn't have a fight with your father." And we said, "Oh, God, I must be wrong."

Then we had imaginary playmates, and people said, "Shut up about that," but that really was our spirit guide, and we didn't know what to do about it. If you're precognitive, you may fear that you're going to be wrong, so you don't want to say it aloud. Then after the fact, don't you want to kick yourself? "I knew that. I knew that, I knew that." After the fact, you don't want to say, "I knew that," because that sounds fake.

I've had my own peers, for that matter, saying to me, "My God, Sylvia, if you make everybody psychic, then where will you be?" *It would make everybody caring and spiritual.* Then we will all be happy, won't we? We will certainly not have to go to a psychic to find out if you have a lot of evil and negativity around you.

Another absolutely bogus thing that keeps people frightened is curses. We still, in this enlightened day, find people who believe in them. Even in Los Angeles, people are coming in and asking, "Sylvia, do you see a curse on me?" I want these poor people to report the fraudulent fortune teller who implanted this idea in them to the district attorney, but they won't. Fear, or better yet, ignorance, makes people give tens of thousands of dollars to such frauds.

It's the same with crystals or with pyramids—they are a fad. I don't mean that there is no validity to these symbols of power, which were used in Atlantis but, please, exercise moderation. Don't hurt yourself by hanging pounds and pounds of rocks around your neck.

Sometimes I wear the dove, which is the sign of Novus Spiritus; sometimes I wear the Star of David; and sometimes I wear the Muslim symbol for Allah, just depending upon what I feel like at that time. I love all these symbols, and I realize that God loves them all, too.

People are identified by: Where do you work? What is your religion? How much money do you make? Where do you live? What kind of house do you live in? What car do you drive? What is your Social Security number? Why don't we approach people as loving, caring entities the way God does? Please note that God cannot have a favorite religion. *Religion* means "dogmatic rules." Now, of course, you need rules that follow the universal consciousness. The best of these is known under many names and in most religions—I know it as the Golden Rule: "Do unto others as you would have them do unto you."

This has a wonderful edge to it. The more you love God, the

less you would ever harm others. People may lie about you, write about you, throw stones at you; but all you ever have to do is stand before God. The only thing that can be judged between you and God is your *motive*.

God's mercy, love, forgiveness, and kindness are always present. They can never, never not be there for you; there is nothing so horrible that you could do.

Francine says, "Auras, which are the emanation of your spirituality, are a direct pipeline to God." Direct pipeline. That energy is never cut off. We may use that pipeline because we're too stupid to know that it exists, but it's always flowing toward us. All you have to do is say, "I know it's there," and the rush comes.

We don't want karmic retribution; I hate that concept. But we're going to live the best life we possibly can. However, I do know that for some reason, if I do anything off-kilter, I get it back so fast that I don't know what happened.

But you see, what we don't realize is that true karma simply means experiencing for the soul. This means you have to examine a person's intent. In other words, I had to hit you intentionally with a mallet for there to be karma. You see what I'm saying? If I bump into you and you fall over, but I'm terribly sorry and I didn't mean it, then there is no karma. But even if I hit you on purpose, karma doesn't mean you should let me have it in the next lifetime. That could go on forever.

If we live our lives with purity and goodness and right motives, we come together, we try to help everyone that we can, we try to help the people with AIDS and the street people, and we go to the convalescent hospitals, what more is there?

Not much more, except to keep trying to give help and to have some kind of place where people can come in and say, "Whew, I'm not judged. No one throws rocks at me here."

What has the world created? We condemned women to lives of horrible marriages, and men, too, for that matter, because we said you can't divorce. Jesus said, "What God has joined together, let no man put asunder." Did anyone stop to think that he meant the intellect and emotion of yourself, male and female within one body?

You see, we're not fighting drugs; we're not fighting against nuclear weapons; we're not fighting ghettos or racial prejudice. *We're fighting ignorance.* That is where the fight goes on.

As I've said before, "We give our lives away to everyone. I give my physical body away to my doctor, I give my finances away to my CPA, I give my freedom away to my lawyer, I give my soul away to my minister, and pretty soon I walk around and say, 'Who am I?'"

We've got to stop that, and we have got to rein it in. We start believing that I'm the father of, the mother of, the daughter of, the sister of . . .

Who are you? Look in your mirror tonight and ask yourself this question. You're not just somebody's spouse or parent. You're an exact mirror image of your Maker.

MEDITATION—COMPLETE REJUVENATION

I want you to put your hands upward on your thighs. This allows you to receive grace. I want you to put the White Light of the Holy Spirit around you. The White Light is nothing more than an emblem of your belief in purity and the Holy Spirit. Then around this I want you to put a purple light, which means higher spirituality. This color is what emanates, because colors can resound with certain attitudes and frames of mind. Then around that, the green light, which means self-healing. Then around that I want you to put the gold, which is also higher consciousness and reaching up for your own spirituality and your own psychic ability.

I want you to feel the infusion and the quiet. Nothing, now, at this point, will disturb you. Relaxation is coming up through the bottoms of your feet, as a complete rejuvenation begins. I want you to feel this energy moving all through you from the Holy Spirit, from Mother God and Father God. You know that God is omnipresent now. God is the Guardianship of Your Mind.

The energy continues to flow through your shoulders, your upper arms, your lower arms, your hands, and your fingertips. Even up now through your neck, around your mouth, your nose, your eyes, and your forehead. I want you to feel with each breath that you exhale that God is present. God omnipotently, creatively perfect, Prima Mobilae, the Unmoved Mover. The omnipotent creative force of God that has always been and always will be, is now present within your soul. Feel the top of your head opening up to Divine intervention.

While you feel that there is an opening, I want you to go through every system of your body. Even if you don't know what they are, let us go through them anyway.

Let us calm down your nervous system. Ask that your nervous system calms down, because we want to have a well body so that we can go about and do God's work.

Feel this relaxation, this healing going right through the upper respiratory area of the body so that we're eager to breathe. Open up the bronchial area and the upper and lower lung area, now going into the digestive area quieting the digestive tract, healing any disruption in the digestion, upper and lower digestive stomach area and intestinal tract. This isn't to rule out any valid pain that's a warning signal. Go right down into the reproductive system, making the right hormonal balance, male and female, so we feel better.

Moving down the central chakras of the body, the pineal and pituitary glands, the pancreas, the thyroid, and our reproductive system, making sure that our chakras are lined up with a brilliant green light, purple light, gold light, and white light so that we immediately feel better than we have ever felt. Now going through the whole liver and pancreatic area, the kidney area, and releasing any and all toxicity in the body, asking for help, demanding help from our own God-Center as well as the God-without.

We have both. We have the linkup and the marvelous

channel to God, and we also carry a part of God so we're emi-
nently protected. Also ask for the archetypes and your guides
to be standing as sentinel figures along the way. I want you
to feel this tremendous elevation of your soul, mind, and spirit.

Now, think of yourself in a field; see and sense it. You're
in a long, flowing robe. The breeze is blowing against your
face and taking care of all the grief, rejection, and hostility, and all the physical or mental molestation that you might
have gone through in this life or any past life, and any
holdovers that you might have carried with you. The fear of
snakes, bridges, burning, feelings of being out of control—
whatever they might be, release them all. Release even what
you don't know. Ask for God to come in and clear all the
cobwebs, all the dark places.

Ask for enough courage to help your friends and loved
ones who are sick. That we're here to hold each other's hand
and help each other until we all graduate. In this field, I want
you to say that you want all the negativity that you might
have inside of yourself to form in front of you, such as low
estimation or judgment. Put them all in front of you like
blocks that keep piling upon blocks. Make them come as large
and as big and as tall as they wish.

Then I want you to feel that all of a sudden beside you
is a large golden sword. This is a representation of your soul
fighting all the adversity that you had to face in life. With
this golden sword, you walk over and take a chop at these
blocks of adversity and poor self-image and all the prejudice
and all the wrongs and all the criticism and all the non-
protection you have endured. You begin to smash these
tremendous blocks that you have in front of you that you
have had to wait and crawl through so that your life can be
all happy and productive.

Now that you have smashed these, you wave the Golden
Sword. All of a sudden, directly out of the clouds above you,
you feel a lightning bolt of power imbued with God's enlight-

enment. You lift the sword, and it goes right down the whole body. You feel shaken to your very roots, and you're all right now. Feel God's whole being encompass you, and feel God's whole being touch you. God is there to touch you, God is there to love you, God is there to heal you, and God is there to give consent to you today. God is there to give consent of your beautiful soul that now shines more prevalent than it has ever been, glorious in its present purification.

Make a promise to yourself once and for all that you won't allow anyone ever again to walk upon you, to hurt you, or to slight you. You have a Golden Sword, and you stand in a field, all trouble gone from you, smiling, triumphant, with God's grace descending and a golden mist around you.

Begin to bring yourself up. Begin to bring yourself back feeling better than you have ever felt, with energy coming up the bottoms of your feet, your ankles, your calves, your knees, your thighs, and your buttocks area. All through the whole trunk, all up through your neck, your face, around your mouth, your nose, your eyes, and your shoulders, your upper arms, your lower arms, your hands, your fingertips. Bring yourself up, all the way up, feeling absolutely marvelous, better than you ever have before.

If during this meditation you felt yourself get teary, please don't be concerned about that. It just means you went very deep. The rest of you who didn't, don't feel bad about that. Some people go so deep that you begin to cry and tears begin to fall, because it's such an emotional release. You want to get to the point that you release that deeply. Not all the meditation in the world can do that until you finally reach that God-Centered place.

That's your temple, as many have said, a beautiful inner Light that was always meant to be there. Don't let anybody spoil it. Don't let anybody tell you what to do and where to go with it, because you're the one who's going to give love and beauty out.

A Gnostic is a seeker of knowledge. A Gnostic isn't going to believe something just because someone says so. You're going to read about it, look it up, and figure it out for yourself. God is pure intellect. So we must approach God through knowledge and wisdom, and stick with that.

People can't negate you when you speak from a point of reason and knowing. You just know it in your own heart that you're a seeker of truth. You don't have to go stomping around, handing out pamphlets. All that does is put a shadow on your soul, and it doesn't let you be enriched. It cuts God off. God isn't able to come in because you're so busy being negative.

That's why we must use our own logic, reason, and thought processes. I tell people everywhere I go, "This philosophy isn't for people who won't think. It will never be for the people who want to be scared to death. It won't be for everybody." And that's okay.

When you have a thinking group, when you rise above ignorance, then you don't deal with all the pettiness of the human condition. You don't have to worry about all that stuff. You just hold a service, you have a healing group, and you all sit around and have a wonderful time. You all love each other, you hug, you give love back and forth, and you each give the other consent to be. That's what it was all meant to be for.

So the reason for us to come together and say, "Oh, you believe the way I believe; oh, there is somebody else here," is that we feel this warmth that begins to exude from each other. We have found a little bit of home.

Forgiveness

If you can't forgive something, give it to God. There are certain things, as I've said in my seminars, that are far beyond our power to forgive.

So, it's perfectly all right to say, "God, I can't forgive that mother who killed her two kids, so I will give it to You"; that's okay.

Then there are those things that you can't forgive yourself for. However, everybody's life has a track that no one can intercept. You were meant to do certain things and follow that path—as hard as it was, as miserable as it was, as much loss as you may have gone through, as much suffering as you may have gone through. Be proud of yourself that you're even walking around. There is something to be said for the fact that we even get up each morning and keep going.

It's too easy on the Other Side, where everything is perfect and we're having a great time, to say, "Give me two rotten kids and an abusive husband," or whatever. "I will take it all," we say, because we're happy.

Then we get down here, and we say, "Wait a minute. I want to cancel this now." Sorry; the contract holds. Now you ask, "Wasn't I stupid?"

No, not really, although we joke about it; you were not stupid. You know what you did? You purposely made your chart difficult because you said, "I want to make it tough so I perfect fast." Gnostics have always done that.

Our lineage of Gnosticism traces back to 7210 B.C.E., through the Templars, the Cathars, and even part of the Masons. Guess what the big hidden secret was? The fact that we knew there was a *Mother God*. America is the only culture that has a problem with this fact. What I find amazing is that logic *dictates* that there is a feminine side; there has to be. Everything in nature is reproduced in doubles. We're made in the image and likeness of God. If you read Genesis [1:26], it says, "Let *us* make mankind in *our* image . . ." Whether you're reading the King James, Douay, Jerusalem, or Aquarian Bible, "us" is used repeatedly in the first book of Genesis— multiple, duality. Go home and check it.

We believe in the Mother God. Father God being static, all loving and all perfect, holds us, but She is the Great Interceptor. She is the One Who creates miracles because She is free to roam, so to speak. All down through history in other countries, whether She was Shiva, whether She was Sophia, whether She was Isis, whether She was Theadora, She was always the Creator, the One Who created originally, and the One Who can create miracles. She is the only One Who can intercept our chart. In other words, if you're meant to have something happen, She is the *Miracle* Worker. Your chart can be modified by Her. The Feminine Principle is an interfering principle. The Mother God can intercede in our lives.

Yes, of course, charts are all written down, but She can actually make changes. He can't. *Intellect* can't move; emotion moves. Consider this: We're an emotional planet, and we have an emotional Mother God who is in residence on this planet.

I love the phrase that follows—so many people make a big deal about this. When Jesus was on the cross and he said, "Mother, behold thy son," he *wasn't* talking to Mary. He was talking to Azna; this is what Francine told me. Current research concludes that Mary could not have been at the crucifixion. Francine said that he looked *up* and said, "Mother, behold thy son," meaning he was speaking to the Mother God. It's that simple. Then at the end when he said, "Father, why hast thou forsaken me?" he was talking to his Father.

The Dead Sea Scrolls uphold this, saying that Mary wasn't even in attendance there. I would really recommend that you read Elaine Pagels' *Gnostic Gospels* (Vintage Books, 1989), because these gospels were some of the books removed at the first Council at Nicaea. These books make Jesus even more loving and human than the New Testament shows.

What's more, why do we want to have a "devil"? We've got enough mean people, enough dark souls running around. We see them on the news, and we work with them. Why do we have to have somebody in a red suit?

People constantly come up to me and say, "Well, you know, there has to be the antithesis to God." No. God is all-loving, all-knowing, all-caring, omnipotent. Every religion believes that, isn't that true?

You sit down with a group of people from every religion and say to them, "Is God all love?"

"Yes," they reply.

"Is God all-knowing?"

"You bet," agree all.

"Is God perfect?"

"Absolutely." All heads nod in agreement.

Then how did God create "bad"? Now, it's true that there are entities with dark souls. What happens is, all of us had the same chance, and some chose to become dark and move away from God. But even at that, the dark entities will eventually be absorbed back into God, in the Uncreated Mass, and purified there. It's all a big plan, don't you see? We need to have negative obstacles so we can test our soul.

Gnosticism always has been logical, if you read, if you think. When somebody tells me they have read the Bible, I ask which of the 26 versions? If they read the King James version, they will miss some 13 books missing found in other translations. If you really want to read the Bible, then read the George Lamsa translations. He did his work directly from the original Aramaic writings.

Many didn't believe that I could get a church established without a fear mechanism. But can we love God rather than fear Him? I love the commandment, "Don't have false gods before Me."

To this day, I still have clients on the phone saying to me, "I think God hates me." That can't be possible. *You* hate you. God doesn't hate. Someone once told me that she didn't believe in God, and I said, "That's okay. God believes in *you*."

I have a friend, Warren, whom I dated when we were both 16 years old in Kansas City, Missouri. We are long-term friends. He always tells the story of this one time when we were walking and I was arguing religion with him, because he was such an egghead. At one point, I was holding my hands up, saying, "All things good come from God," and a bird pooped into my hand, which turned out to be foretelling my life. He always told that story with glee.

So I went to see Warren as he was getting ready to die from liver cancer; the doctor had given him ten days. He turned over on his side, big-eyed.

I said, "I'm so mad at you."

He said, "I know." And then he said, "Why are you mad at me?"

"Because you're getting to go Home, and I'm not."

Then he said, "Okay, *now* tell me how death will be."

I said, "It has taken me 40-some odd years to get you to listen to me, and finally you are ready to hear it?!"

So he said, "How will it go?"

This is where Gnostics really come in handy because we go everywhere, so I said, "You will have a tunnel come out of your body, and another tunnel will come toward you. When it does, you will see an opening about the size of—"

"What size?" he interrupted, ever the engineer and attorney, you know.

I said, "I don't know, 18 inches, what the hell. Then the tunnel gets bigger and bigger, and then you move toward it."

And he said, "Then what?"

I said, "A Being of Light will meet you. It could be a grandmother, your guide, an angel, an old friend, or many other loved ones."

He said, "Really? What will I do then?"

I said, "You will go to the Hall of Wisdom and scan your life. No one will judge you, as people do here, but you will say, 'Oh, there were a few things I could have done better,' and, 'Damn, why did I do *that?*' But you will learn from the experience. Besides, everybody today, on the Other Side, is watching what we do. They watch us all the time, and they also learn from what we do. So we're not just a congregation of people here. There is a congregation of souls who watch us. So will you be able to watch after your loved ones."

He said, "How will I get out?"

I said, "Warren, you're a pilot, you know what it's like at liftoff?"

He said, "Sure I do."

"Well, you take three deep breaths, and you lift off." I walked out, and I sat with his wife for a while and talked to her. I get home, and she calls me; she didn't know what Warren and I had talked about.

She said, "I don't know what happened. I went in there, and he was taking these deep breaths and he left. He just lifted off."

❦ ❦ ❦

A Prayer to God

Dear God,

Forgive us for what we have done to ourselves.
Forgive us for what we have listened to and absorbed
and how we lost our way and didn't realize that You were
inside of us all the time. Protect us, Dear God, throughout
this next year. Let us grow in spirituality, let us grow in
faith of ourselves, and let us love ourselves and others.
Please help us not to take everything so seriously, to be
able to laugh and to have fun and to bring about joy,
and to nourish and nurture and care about ourselves.
Dear God, we ask this in the name of the Father, the Son
and the Holy Spirit, feeling bright, rejuvenated, full
of love, caring and peace with resolution.

❦ ❦ ❦

Your one resolution is that you will love yourself, and in doing so, you will be able to love other people.

❦ ❦ ❦

Gnosticism is back in full swing. Every time the movement has risen, it has been beaten down. This time it won't be; I'm convinced of that. I said to a really good friend of mine, "You know, if it's a pink dog with spots and the person believes in it, for God's sake, stand for it. If you're Lutheran, then be a good one; if you're Episcopalian, then be a good one; if you're Catholic, be a good one. But don't waffle." If you're Gnostic, then be a good one, but don't waffle.

Our tenets are beautiful. Everything in the tenets of our church is loving, giving, caring, supportive, and in defense of the family. Everything is about love.

You say, "Oh, that's too easy." No, it isn't; it's hard. Because there are certain people you don't want to love, but you have to love their soul. But you certainly don't have to live with them, and you don't have to be around them. What you do is you say, "I hope you know God loves you; I do. Now go away," and wish them well.

What you must do is profess. Really profess what you believe in and stand tall within it; truly live what you believe. I guess what most people have a problem with is the Mother God concept. We always hear we're made in the image and likeness of God. Then so am I, as a woman, made in the image and likeness of God. Men are, too. Women also know that we have an intellectual and emotional side to our brain; a feminine and male side. So where does the female side come from? All of a sudden God decides to make this strange phenomenon called a woman? No, the image already existed.

Some people are furious with us because we want to resurrect the feminine side. We don't mean ruling you males out, but we're talking about bringing up the feminine side, which is the nurturing side. That's what Jesus was—the nurturer, the giver of love.

Sure, he also had righteous anger; that's why he took a whip to the people in the temple. He wasn't a wimp. Did you ever notice when he said, "The meek shall inherit the Earth"? If you're going to be a wimp, all you're going to get is this physical world. He had a wonderful sense of humor.

MEDITATION—THE LIGHT OF GOD'S GRACE AND LOVE

Put your hands upward on your lap and uncross your legs. Let us call on the white light of the Holy Spirit, on our angels, and on our guides. The whole room is now filled with the light of our angels, Mother God who walks among us, and Father God who holds us. The Holy Spirit, like a silver mantle, descends upon all of our hearts, souls, and minds. For this coming week and for the weeks that follow, we ask that the Holy Spirit move within us. We ask for the protection of Light. We ask for the forgiveness of ourselves. We ask for the enhancement of our whole God-Consciousness and the Divinity of our soul, because we're from the greatest genetics anywhere in the universe. We're singular, and we're experiencing for God—bad, good, indifferent. We're asking for the Holy Light to shine upon us, and for the love of God to embrace us.

Scanning back through all of our past lives, let us release any and all karma. Let us not get caught in someone else's karma. Singularly and collectively, we're like golden beads threading through. Each and every one of us is part of that golden bead necklace that hangs around the neck of God— each individual, each glistening, each perfect in its own right. Bring down the holiness and the infusion and the steadfastness that we will stick together through everything, that we're a unit, that we're an arrow that pierces through darkness, that no darkness can ever assail us because we're together—maybe in a dark world, but we are a Light.

We are a Light, a haven, that says, "Come and we will give you peace, we will give you harmony, we will give you forgiveness, and we will give you love. You that are filled with God's Light, we welcome all of you."

When you come in, leave all your negative junk at the door. Leave all of the "I should have dones," and "I didn't dos," and "I wish I hads," and "I could have dones." Let it go today. You did what only you could do, and you held up the best that you could hold up. God permanently, forever, infinitely, loves you. We ask for grace; we ask that our grace emanates and fills up the room and spreads out over us, like warm, golden honey down the aisle of our life. The beautiful figures of Mother Azna, God the Father, and all messiahs come; so wherever we meet, wherever we are, we are attended to. Our angels stand in glowing robes, surrounding us, holding on to us, embracing us, and loving us. We ask for the grace of God in the name of the Father, the Son, the Mother, and the Holy Spirit. Amen.

Bring yourself up, all the way up. We are linked together for all eternity. God love you and keep you safe.

Chapter Seven

GNOSTIC CHRISTIANITY

Sylvia: The Gnostic movement loves God, and we respect each person's path toward knowing God.

Novus believes that any question asked can be answered. There is no need to rely upon blind faith alone. Just as God gave us an inquiring mind, so too did he give us the means to resolve its questions. We appeal to those who need an intellectual basis for God, not to those who are afraid to think and never question the basis of their beliefs.

We believe that you come back into life many, many times. God gives you opportunities to be everything that you want to be and to perfect your soul for God. This religion is based on knowledge, truth, understanding, and reason. You've got to find your way back to your own truth. That's what the word *Gnosis* means: knowledge.

We also believe that when you die, you go to the Other Side, which is a marvelous, beautiful place that's superimposed upon this Earth and stands about three feet above our ground. That's why many times when you will see spirits, they seem to be floating above the ground. In actuality, they're walking on their own ground level.

In the beginning of Gnosticism, which Jesus was a part of, all 18 tenets were known. This was the earliest of all possible religions, with one defining difference. They believed in the duality of Mother and Father God. We know that we're male and female within ourselves—intellect and emotion. Why is it so hard to believe that there could be a feminine Divinity?

The sad part of today's Christianity is that everybody has forgotten God the Father. That's exactly what Jesus was trying to restore, to help us remember our loving Father in heaven. In his Sermon on the Mount when he said, "Pray like this, 'Our Father who art in Heaven . . . ,'" he didn't say, "Pray to me." When he said, "You must go through me to get to the Father," he meant that his teachings were the path to the Father.

Why do we come together? It rejuvenates us.

Why has church failed? Too judgmental.

But what is church? Church is people.

MEDITATION—GOLD AND PURPLE LIGHT

I want you to sit up straight, put your hands upward on your thighs, and surround yourself with a gold light. Close your eyes, and take a deep breath in. This is your moment to be with God; it makes up for all the other moments of our life. I want you to feel the relaxation coming up through your body. Feel total and complete unity with yourself, exhaling and breathing in deeply.

Feel a gold and purple light around you keeping you from all harm. Of course, white light is always there, but band yourself with color all around and through your body. Nothing disturbs you, and nothing bothers you.

Feel yourself go into a tiny room, small but not closed off. Sit on the floor of this room inside yourself, and feel the presence of the Divine, since you're a spark of the Divine. I want you to feel that room enlarging as if the walls expand. This feeling begins to push upward. The whole room is filled with the Light radiating through every part of your physical being, which is nothing more than a vehicle that's faulty at best. But we're going to keep it running the best we can for as long as we can because it houses our spirit. Let that Light rinse out all the problems of finances, children, in-laws, living situations, fear of the unknown, or fear of being hurt. Let it rinse away all the phobic terrors.

Now begin to bring in your loved ones, one at a time— those whom you wish to protect, those whom you wish would have betterment in their lives, and those whom you wish to heal. Let that Light bathe the sick, the ill, or just people you want to protect, people you want to remember. Bathe them in this gold and purple light with shafts of it illuminating. Feel the omnipresence of yourself and the truth that lies within your own heart—your God-Centeredness, your Gnostic-Centeredness. Feel all the feelings of fear, of antagonism, of revenge begin to drop away. Nothing will hurt you.

Now begin to bring energy up through the very bottoms of your feet and your ankles, just like you relaxed before. Remember this meditation to get closer to God. Move all the way up through the ankles, the calves, the knees, the thighs. Up through the whole trunk of the body, down through the shoulders, the upper arms, the lower arms, the hands, the fingertips. Up through the neck, around the face, the mouth, the nose, the eyes. Bring yourself up, all the way up on the count of three. One, two, three.

Origins

I want you to realize that what I've been discussing is taken from history and from scholarly work. I hope I've been clear about what was infused from Francine and Raheim, and what was researched historically. Gnosticism is nothing that Novus Spiritus made up. This is part of history and part of the written word, and every theological scholar knows this to be true.

The Gnostic religion is what Jesus belonged to. The apostles became Gnostics, which meant they were a free-thinking group, and let us even use the word *ecumenical,* which means "universal."

This is what the *Nag Hammadi* scrolls prove. These Gnostic texts were deliberately put away because they went against "the church." But as always, truth will find a way to be heard. Novus is one of those ways.

In the *Gnostic Gospels,* Elaine Pagels writes, "Since no one of later generation can have access to Christ as the apostles"—this is what the church said during his lifetime at the "resurrection"—"every believer must look to the Church of Rome which they founded and to the Bishop for authority." Some Gnostic Christians contested the Apocalypse of Peter, among the latest writings discovered at Nag Hammadi. They tell how dismayed Peter was to hear that many believers will fall into an erroneous name and will be ruled heretically. The "risen" Jesus explains to Peter that those who name themselves bishops, as if they have received their authority from God, are in reality "waterless channels." "Although they don't understand mystery, they boast that the mystery of truth belongs only to them and to their church alone."

The author then accuses them of having misinterpreted the apostles' teachings and thus having set up an imitation church in the place of the true Christian brotherhood that was the Gnostic religion.

No one can ever say to you that Gnosis is a mystery, not in my religion.

Francine said, "Anything that you can ask can be answered, if you could think of the questions." This made me crazy at first, because then you wonder what you haven't asked. But to say that God is a mystery, that life after life is a mystery, that the Trinity is a mystery—that's nonsense. There is no mystery; there is just nobody asking the right questions.

Don't you see what a mystery does? It makes you dependent; it makes us all idiots; and then only one person has the knowledge. You can seek knowledge within your own heart. You are your own temple. You're your God-Consciousness. You are the Holy Spirit that moves in the world. Don't let anyone rule you, because that's dangerous. That's what happens in cults.

We can never judge another's soul, although we must react rationally to actions created by others. In any life, how do we know we haven't been murderers and cheats and burglars and whatever? People don't like to believe that, but I've got documentation to prove it. Boy, do I know about lives in which people thought they were saintly. We have all done everything, and some of us had a good time while doing it.

This is a very human church, a very human religion. Isn't that how it should be? Aren't we human? Aren't we part of God? Why have we always chafed against that? What are the rules supposed to be—that you never have a wicked thought? That you never coveted something? That you're not human?

Simply try to be the best you can, but we're human. God understands our humanness. If you take the humanness away from us, then you're going to take away the emotion, and that's the very reason we're here. God must experience through our emotions. We know what that's about, don't we? Everyone who has ever tried to bring love and take out the humanness of God, Who can't be human, is subject to ridicule. The only part of God that's human is *us*.

Why does love make people so mad? I'm not just talking about a certain group of people. I'm talking about anybody who gets the literal word and doesn't go any further with it. Why does it make people so angry when I say, "We're going to love God and follow in the ways that Jesus taught"? It makes people mad, so they say, "You must be a cult." There is nothing more occult than some religions: They tell you what to do, they tell you how to live, they tell you what to eat, and they tell you who you can be with.

I never will forget when I was 18 years of age, I was going steady with a boy named Joe. I went to confession, and as I was sitting in the confessional like a good Catholic girl, I said, "I'm going steady."

The priest said, "You're going steady. You know what that leads to?" I said, "No." I wasn't being naive; I just didn't know what he was talking about. He said, "Well, it leads to sexuality." I said, "I don't think going steady does that." With that he said—listen to this—"I'm not giving you absolution," and he shut the grate. This is a *very* serious condemnation to Catholics.

I went back out to my boyfriend, just destroyed, and told him about it. The next thing I knew, Joe was up at the priest's door banging on the door screaming at the top of his lungs, "How dare you refuse absolution to my girlfriend."

The priest said, "Oh, well, I just had a bad day. Come in, and I will give her absolution."

Now listen to this, at this point, I said, "I don't want to be absolved now, because now I'm mad." True story, but then I began to think: *How can this man absolve me of anything, when I can go directly to God?*

Believe me when I tell you, I think priests are marvelous, because they really can be like psychiatrists. It's something within the human nature that makes us want to repent and ventilate, don't we? It seems like we have to get it off our chest; it's a known fact. I will say this: Catholics go to psychiatrists less, and I think it's because of confession.

The danger in organized religion happens when you say, "Let somebody else think for me. Let somebody else tell me what's right and what isn't. Let's have somebody else define sin, and then I will be saved." Don't be spiritually lazy. I can give you all the information that I've read, but you should look it up and check it out by yourself.

How do we know if something is bad or good? As Raheim said, "It's how you feel inside."

Always, regardless of which religion I was in, something in me yearned for more truth. Something in me yearned for the love of God, not the fear of God. I want to walk around in the blanket of Mother and Father God loving me. I want to know that I'm walking in the path of the God-Consciousness. I don't want to be clouded by all the fear. If I ate meat on one day and then died the next, was I going to go to hell? I don't want that. I don't want that for you, and you don't want that for you.

How do we become more spiritual? As Francine said, "Do a good act for someone." Isn't that simple? A good act every day, kindness and love, but you can't do that when you're clouded with fear. Have you ever noticed that people who are caught up in dogma are mean and judgmental? They judge everybody. I don't understand. Jesus said, "Judge not that ye be not judged."

It's so simple that many can't believe it: Love God, do good, and then shut up and go Home. Why does the human being need so many laws? Why can't we have the freedom to love and to walk in peace?

We're seeing a lift coming, but look at the prejudice against African Americans, against Asians, against Jews, against gays. It's rising in the name of "God." That to me is blasphemous. If there is any blasphemy, there is where it is. Horrifying. I'm afraid we're going to see more of that prejudice again.

Does the same God who moves through me move through every single human being that lives? Yes. Am I a unique part of God? Yes, the same as anybody else. The same part of God links us together. Once you begin to go against your fellow humans in hate, then you've missed the mark. That's the dark side of things—the judgment, the hate, the prejudice, the bigotry. That's where evil abounds, and all in the name of "God." It's scary.

On the *Montel Williams Show,* when I was asked, "So when is Jesus coming again?" I said, "I didn't know he left. He is certainly always within me. Now sit down."

He isn't going to return. He is inside us, in our God-Consciousness. They're all looking up at the sky hoping that he will save them, not realizing that they will have to save themselves.

What does *salvation* mean? It means to save *yourself* from the darkness, the bigotry and the fear. If somebody is creating darkness in your life, say, "I bless you, I put you in the white mantle of the Holy Spirit," and then go away.

"Our journey," people say, "is very long." No, it's very quick. Those of us who are getting to be more mature realize how fast it's going. I want all of us to have enough time to, in some small or large way, take off the crust of fear, to love God and show truly that Jesus didn't live and walk the Earth in vain, that his words will live on through us as Gnostics. That's my mission in life: to bring the Gnostic truth into the world.

MEDITATION—STAR OF TRUTH

Put yourself in the white light of the Holy Spirit and into a velvety, warm, dark night with countless stars. Even though you're standing out on top of a hill, you see this big, huge star suddenly appear right above you, almost like the gigantic ball in Times Square. This massive star seems to be slowly, slowly descending. Then you quickly realize that this star is, like the ball, closing off the old and bringing about the new. With each micrometer that it begins to descend, you release all the anger and all the hostility and all the pain from this last year. We have a lot of it. Let it go on the wind to be taken away from you.

The star slowly descends with the countdown, giving you renewed life, renewed peace, and renewed fortitude and perseverance to go on from this point on with determination and truth. It's so close that you can almost feel its very warm Light. The countdown is zero.

Out of that star walks the Mother God with arms outstretched; behind Her silhouetted is Father God; to the right of Her is the God-Consciousness; and in the form of love that extends from the Mother and Father is the Holy Spirit. You feel Them embrace you, and the truth goes straight into your heart. You're releasing now all the pains and all the pent-up emotions. Anything that has settled in your body to make you ill, release it. Ask for inner sight, inner knowledge. Ask Jesus to enter your heart and give you truth.

He didn't say, "I'm the way, the truth, and the life," but rather, "I will give you the way, the truth and the light."

Feel the power of God invade every cell, making you well in mind, body, and spirit. It's not enough that you should grasp truth only for yourself—but also give it to someone else. Hand this truth to them, whether they accept it or not. If they want to drop it, they have dropped it; but at least you've discharged your duty, getting rid of their pain, their fear, and their guilt that's a killer. It mars the soul and causes a breach of essence.

The star rises again in the sky, and yet you have the warm glow of protection and forgiveness and truth around you. We stick together, we stay together, and we stand firm and tall against defamation and against anything that wants to fell us. We're on a mission, a mission from God to rid the world of guilt and hate and bigotry—to love animals, to love trees, to love children, to give of ourselves to every entity, all living things, part of us, part of our world. We ask that all people who are not with us today and all animals and all children to be surrounded by our love. We ask this in the name of the Mother, the Father, the God-Consciousness, and the Holy Spirit.

Bring yourself up, all the way up, feeling absolutely marvelous, better than you have ever felt. On the count of three, bring yourself all the way up. One, two, three.

The Jesus of History, Not of Faith

The historical records of Jesus are very sketchy. He walked and talked and performed miracles, as reported by the Gospels Matthew, Mark, Luke, John, and later Paul. But the Jesus of history is a man like Siddhartha, who was Buddha, or Mohammed, and did wondrous things and was purported to have said that he was the "Son of God."

The Jesus that has been portrayed by men of faith is another thing entirely. This image became a big, working "church machine." They found a charismatic person and customized his image, not because Jesus was less than he was, but because it brought them money and prestige. It could have been anyone. It could have been his contemporary, Apollonius of Tyana, who was a great and marvelous person who did the exact same things as Jesus. *Think* when I'm saying this. In no way am I tearing Jesus down; I'm just going to show you what churches have done.

In Jesus' day, there were few medical practitioners available in his homeland. Only in the Egyptian community were there any type of physicians. In those times when people were sick, they were turned out into the streets. If you were a lunatic, you were put out on the street. Now enters a man who can *psychically* see and feel and know and heal. What do you think happens?

Jesus never wanted to be deified. He wanted us to always go back to God the Father. He said, "I'm one *of many* that come to preach the truth." He was a Gnostic, the same as we are. Let us go further: Jesus' teachings are opposed to the Old Testament teachings. There is nothing in his words that talks about hellfire, burning, and damnation.

Christian teaching is loving and forgiving. If you're going to follow Jesus, then you have to drop the hate and the judgment. Jesus said it: "You without sin cast the first stone."

In any life, how do we know what we have done in other lives? We could have all been murderers and crucifiers and molesters and all those things. We don't like to believe that, but everybody has a chance to be everything.

You have to know in your heart that God is with you. Every one of you has a spark of Jesus, of Buddha, of Mohammed.

The minute somebody says, "I have all the answers," they immediately try to make you subservient to them. There again you are leaving your salvation to someone else. The churches promoted this idea, then began to grind out these fears and horrors, and they began to decide many things that Jesus never said. Jesus was the champion of personal salvation and reliance upon the self. He told people to ignore the church rules and seek God on their own terms. He never set rules nor morality edicts, other than to love God and love one another.

Why should I let someone tell me whether my love for God, that's going directly to God, is appropriate or not? How can they? Your love for God and your very soul is unique unto yourself. Your spark of God is different from my spark, but your spark with all the other sparks make up the totality. Each one of us is unique.

If we all were to witness an event and we all wrote about it, as I used to do with my students in grade school, do you know how different every account would be? It's not because each person is wrong, but everyone sees things through their own experiences and from their own perspective. The church was built by people with their own view of Jesus.

In being a Gnostic, no one can ever shake you, don't you see? You never have to say to anyone that you believe simply "on faith," because you *know* it. It's in your heart and in your God-Centeredness, and then you can rise up and respond. They don't know about the Nag Hammadi and the Dead Sea Scrolls; those were the lost teachings eradicated by the church. The Dead Sea Scrolls go into reincarnation, the auras, the enlightenment of the soul, and every man being his own Kingdom of Heaven.

You shouldn't come to church to be saved, but to share your salvation with like-minded people. You're going to evolve to the point where things won't hurt you and bother you. You may say, "Well, I should go out and talk to people." No, don't do that. Don't convert unwilling people. I don't want them, do you? Yes, I want our church to grow, but let people come to you and ask about it, then give them everything you know and feel.

MEDITATION—RELEASING

Surround yourself today and always with white light. I also want you to use a brilliant orange light, and feel it ema-

nating from the top of your head right into the chest area. Let it stay in the chest area for quite a while, and then seep down to the solar plexus. The orange light cleanses out the hurt in your heart and the pain in your solar plexus that comes from being abused, bruised, and hurt; it keeps you warm inside. Starting at the top of your head, let it run like paint inside and out. Orange, beautiful, brilliant, luminescent paint—a thick, luxurious feeling of orange streaming down to the waist. You're bathed in it inside and out; it protects you from being hurt in the solar plexus. Many of us, when we take a blow, take it right in the solar plexus, in the heart chakra. Ease the heart, and don't let your heart be broken.

From the waist down, I want you to feel and see green, a gorgeous pulsating emerald green like the Emerald City of Oz. Green is a growing, cathartic color. Everything that's toxic will be rinsed away, flushing out any and all negativity. The orange has pushed it to the lower extremities, and the green is flushing it away down through the lower intestinal tract, the buttocks, down through the legs and out the feet. It dissipates. Then the color widening around you begins to whirl and spin and cleanse. All the dark smoke that emanates from you is cleansed away.

Construct around you a pyramid as big as you so that you can stand inside. On the top of this pyramid is a lavender crystal. As the sun hits this lavender crystal, it becomes more purple and begins to turn and rotate. You can feel the emanation of this spirituality. Inside the crystal, construct a pyramid, a light-form that's upside down with the "V" in the middle of your forehead and open at the top. The spinning purple of the crystal pushes the light down through the open-funneled pyramid right through the crown chakra of your head, through the whole and complete being that is you, cleansing and healing.

With each breath you exhale, you let go of all the pain,

the suffering, the loss, the grief, the rejection. Let it go. Exhale, and let it go. No one can hurt you again. No one can make you be anything you're not, because you're a perfect unit. You're not a "sinner." If you're a sinner, then God is full of sin, and that can't be possible. You may have done a wrong, but most of the time that's against yourself. Forgive yourself for any wrongdoing you have done to yourself.

Bring energy right up through the bottoms of your feet, your ankles, your calves, your knees, your thighs, the buttocks area, the trunk of the body; and down through the shoulders, the upper arms, the lower arms, the hands, and the fingertips. Count to three and bring yourself out, all the way out, feeling absolutely marvelous, better than ever before. One, two, three.

A Church to Discern Truth

I want to take you on a journey that goes way back, over 7,000 years. This can all be validated by reading and research. From the first recorded history that we have, there were always women prophets and psychics—in Egyptian times, Mesopotamian, Sumerian, always. Then there was a short time in which there were male prophets, but the oracles in Greece were primarily women. The astrologers, however, were men of the court. If modern religion hadn't become so patriarchal, it would have been balanced between both sexes.

After Moses took the people out of Egypt, they decided they were going to have a patriarchal religion. This was a direct rebuttal to the Egyptians, who had many female goddesses. Moses wasn't about to have any part of that, and that's why you read in Exodus, "Don't suffer a witch to live." Here is another example of a bad translation. In the original Aramaic, the actual word was "poisoner," not "witch."

You notice that whenever the *male* prophets speak, it's all right—

that's perfectly psychic and valid. Whether it was Daniel or Elijah, they could all speak about coming events, but women could not. In the first book of Samuel, when the "Witch" of Endor calls up Samuel [28:7], no one says anything about that, because she could speak and she could channel. Do you notice that is the last time in the Bible anything is said about a female prophet, except in the Book of Judges, and then just briefly, about Debora? So even the males stopped prophesying.

If you notice, from the Old Testament Book of Judges, to the New Testament, there are no prophets except Jesus. Of course Jesus was a prophet, and he was psychic. How do you suppose he knew when someone had seizures, and that they were epileptic? Then he said, "And now you will sleep." How do you suppose he knew all that stuff? He had medical knowledge. Because of his power—to his disappointment—Christianity eventually became even more patriarchal.

Don't you see that if you all become psychics, you're not going to need anyone to give you direction? You won't need priests—only each other.

We're coming into an age now where the psychic and spiritual cannot be separated. It wasn't separate in our Lord, and it wasn't with any great teacher in this world. You can't separate it. What do you think Our Lady of Fatima was? It was a vision all down through the world. It hasn't been only the Catholics who have had visions.

There is one simple key to developing your psychic ability: You must take your first impression, the first thing that comes into your mind, and build on it. Don't say to yourself, "That isn't logical," because nothing psychic is. It's the first thrust that comes through, and keep your analytical mind quiet.

Give yourself up to it. It's the only way to live. It's the only lifeline you have down here. It's your only calling card. Do not separate yourself from that Divine intervention and that coursing power that runs from God to you. Religion hasn't made anybody better. Your soul, your striving through life, is what makes you better, life after life.

Real Meaning

We are often tested to see how much we will give of ourselves, the love, the support, the help. Once, my parishioners and I went to a retirement community to sing and give out little presents. As we walked down the aisle, I saw one of the parishioners really being affected by the physical and mental plight of some of the people there, so I ran up to her right away and said, "For God's sake, put the white light of the Holy Spirit around you."

Those elderly people were grabbing our hands. One woman thought that I was her dead daughter who had come back; that just about did me in. I let her go on thinking it; you bet I did. She said, "You're dead, and I didn't think you could come back."

I said, "You knew I would come back."

It dawned on me, going through this group, that the first thing that comes to your mind—no matter how much you know—is, "Why would an all-loving God allow this, regardless of our chart? Why would we even write a chart that includes such suffering?"

First of all, as I've said so many times, we don't know what that person is proving—maybe, if nothing else, to be a symbol by which others change their lives. More important, it became clear exactly how vital we are to each other. We're each a part of the Divine God of love.

Rather than looking around screaming at God, "Where are you? Why don't you answer my prayer?," it's up to each and every one of us to answer someone else's prayer. We're the active, emotional part of God that must react and do something.

A rabbi once told me this wonderful story: A man dies and meets God in heaven. The man says, "There is so much suffering and pain in the world. Why don't you send help." God replied, "I did send help. I sent *you*."

I've always said, "Hey, God, you take care of me, and I will take care of as many as I can." What thanks or benefit is there except one human being caring for another?

Spirituality is all about getting out there and helping each other.

The one thing that has kept me well is the White Light and what my grandmother used to say to me, "Your life is going to be terribly hard, but Sylvia, remember one thing: Within your weakness, there lies your strength sleeping."

People say, "If I'm doing for everyone else, then I don't have any time for myself." What do you mean? You never get away from yourself. Don't you live in there? Of course you do, and it better be comfortable to live in there. You better like what you feel inside of yourself. Living a spiritual life will ensure that *you* are content with *you*.

In the morning, you should get up and say to God, "This day is for You," because it makes the day so much easier, regardless of what adversity you will face.

Does God need that? Of course He doesn't—God is perfect and omnipotent, but *your* God-Center needs that because we are in human form. Being separate from that Divine Love and God-Consciousness is deadly. That's where despair comes in, where depression comes in, and where negativity comes in. Negativity, avarice, greed, consciously trying to hurt another person—any evil that exists in this world, is part of the physiological makeup of the human being that we must all overcome.

"When we come into life," as Francine says, "the flesh creates the greed, the avarice, the calumny, the scandal, the backbiting, the hurt."

When it gets so bad that you think you can't pull it together anymore and that you just can't survive, something comes to relieve you. We've all had to endure the deaths of loved ones, and we might go through more. We can have public ridicule, or we can have all our personal property ripped away from us. But does it all really matter? No. You get to the point where you say, "What else can they do?" Not much. *It tempers the soul.* It makes you strong. It makes you stand taller with the pride of surviving.

The 12 days of Christmas begin on December 14. During that period, or anytime when you need rejuvenation, make a commitment within yourself to do something kind. Call someone whom you don't necessarily get in touch with, but who you feel needs cheering up. One of my ministers, Michael, stopped on the highway and picked up a woman and her mother and a child because they had a flat tire. I know you don't want to be running around helping people on lonely roads because it's dangerous, especially for women, but there are people within our own neighborhood and within our families whom we should extend a hand to.

You will be surprised at how wonderful you feel—even to the point of keeping your mouth shut when your mother—or your child—says something that makes you want to scream.

Most of all, be good to you. Every day, do one good act for yourself. Give yourself 12 Christmas presents. Go get your hair done; buy something new for yourself. Treat yourself to just sitting in front of the TV and watching it all day if you want, or read a good book, or stay up later than you usually do and not worry about it. Think of yourself as being in love with *you*. You have to love yourself. Think about how much God loves you—that alone makes you worth loving.

Dear God,

*We ask You for enlightenment, to be able to heal, to be
able to give your word out, to give strength, to maintain
peace of mind that will stay in our hearts forever.
Beloved Father, we ask to send healing grace to all the
people who need our help, all the people who are named
in our hearts, and even those people that are nameless to
us. Whether they're poor; deprived; in a foreign country;
on the street; persecuted by race, creed or religion—
we ask for Your help and blessing for everyone.
That's our present—a Gold Light, giant fingers of gold into
every heart that needs it. More important, Lord, that they
accept Your Divine Light and Your comfort and Your
peace, and the feeling and knowledge of the will to go on.*

We ask to finish this life and be proud of what we
have done. Just like in school, to be a helper, student
helper, teacher helper. We add our hands, our
shoulders, our lips to give service to your people.
We ask this in the name of the Father
and the Mother and the Holy Spirit. Amen.

MEDITATION—BLESSINGS TO THOSE IN NEED

Put your hands upward on your thighs, and surround
yourself with gold light. Circulate that gold light like a pin-
wheel over your head, and bring it down all the way through
your entire body. As it goes down your body, have it spiral
back up again, almost like a fan rotating. Take a deep breath
and let it go. Just let God and let go.

Dear Father, Son, Holy Spirit, and Mother God, intellect
and emotion, we ask for Your guidance, we ask for Your help,
and we ask for health. We ask for love and loyalty from all
the people whom we love and give loyalty to. God, we want
you to see our steadfastness and our conviction so that noth-
ing will make us waver from our beliefs. In our beliefs and
our strengths, we ask for financial help to keep going. We
ask that the power be given to us so that we can send our
Light out to everyone else; that we can make a larger pin-
wheel of golden light that turns into many colors of green
light for healing, blue for peace, even a little rosy-red for stim-
ulation; that everyone we know and everyone we love and
all those who are not here (and first and foremost our Gnostic
Christian group) receive healing, love, caring, and especially
the gift of not being lonely.

We then extend this pinwheel of color to all the children
who are neglected, to all the elderly, to all the people on the
street who have no one, to all the races and creeds who have
endured prejudice, to each and every one singularly with

any pain and heartache that they're now experiencing—so any pain is alleviated and neutralized and replaced by grace and strength. No matter what happens with our families or with our homes, we will be steadfast, we will have protection, and we will make this pinwheel of color around us.

We ask for blessings upon each and every one of us and for all those sick and ailing. Even though they don't know our name, we're all brothers and sisters together. Sometimes we have to commit all the way before we get anything back; that seems to be the law. It's like we have to give it all up before we can get it.

Feel the quiet; feel the peace; feel your continued love affair with the Holy Spirit, with God, and with the avatars who have taught us. Feel the total commitment of yourself to your own God-Center. From this time forward, don't let anything knock you down. Our bodies may be crippled or sick, and we may have pressures and stress, but there is nothing anyone can do to hurt our souls—only we can do that. Open up your soul and let it heal. Whatever worries you have, let them heal, and let them be rinsed clear.

We ask this in the name of the Father, the Mother, and the Holy Spirit.

Bring yourself back up to consciousness, feeling absolutely marvelous, better than you have ever felt before. Feel the Thanksgiving and Christmas spirit in your heart.

The Mother Goddess

I'm going to open up, as I am known to do, a can of worms. I'm a mother. I'm so much of a mother that I'm convinced that everyone around me thinks I am "off." I adore my children beyond the point of any reasoning. I know a lot of you mothers share this feeling, especially if you're mothers of sons. But would I do it again? No.

From years of being in the reading room and talking to mothers, it used to be after the tape clicked off that I would say to a mother, "You know how much we love our children, but would you ever do it again?"

We all said in silent whispers, "No," as if God would hear us and do something terrible. I think motherhood is rewarding, but it's also one of the greatest ways to become both a saint and a martyr that anyone knows of. I don't think there is any man in the room who will understand it. Fathers, of course, have a unique and entirely different relationship with their children. But I don't think anyone knows or can possibly know—I'm not even sure, psychically, that one mother can know what goes on with another mother—except we know there is pain and there is worry. Like so many mothers (but unlike fathers) we always thought that at one far-off day, we would get our children raised and we wouldn't worry. Ha, ha, ha. Now I'm convinced that even in the grave, we mothers will worry.

My grandmother used to say, "When they're little, they step on your feet. When they get big, they step on your heart."

I've done it to my parents. We have all done it to our parents, and in turn the cycle goes on. But in the aspect of now that they're here and they're with us, would you give up your life for them? You bet, in a second.

This motherhood theme is so strong that it ruled all ancient religions. It ruled way before the patriarchal theme of just Father God. The Mother God was eulogized and respected and loved, whether it was Isis or Sibyl, far before the time of Jesus. Sibyl was 250 years before the time of Jesus. Sophia, on the other hand, went thousands of years back, so far back that no one can even record it.

With the advent of Judaism, Christianity, and Islam, everything became paternal and the Mother God was ruled out totally. Logically, in your own mind, there can't be such a lopsided God.

We are Gnostics, "Seekers of Truth." The ancient Gnostics believed, as did the Atlanteans, the Sumerians, the Babylonians, and the Egyptians, that there was always a feminine deity, whether it was Mother Nature or the Mother Goddess. It was a very purposeful campaign to rule out the Mother God entirely and bring about a patriarchal religion. Now, as we all know, the "Blessed Mother Mary" has been elevated to the point of being like a "mother god" for Catholics, who are told to pray to her.

Everything today is pointing back to the feminine principle. The patriarchal principle of the vengeful, monotheistic religion has caused so much pain, so much guilt, and so much fear. This is not what God really is; it's only what man has created for political reasons.

No other religion in the Western world has a Mother Goddess except Gnosticism. She is just as powerful and rules this Earth as Father God does. We, as Gnostics, accept the Mother God principle because it's too lopsided if you don't. It doesn't even stand to reason. The reason people have always had a problem with the Mother Goddess concept is because it always belonged to the Wiccans, from which the word *witch* came. "Witches" always believed in just the Mother Goddess, so that has always had a bad connotation. But we commonly speak of Mother Earth and Mother Nature with no negative aspects.

Let's look at the theology of this. God the Father, all-knowing, all intellect, holds us in the palms of His hands. His static energy, His nonchanging force—the conceptual knowledge of us holds us, but there is no emotion there. We are the emotional side of God that's experiencing for God, but we have no principle that "rules" us except the Feminine Principle. *Rule* is a bad word, but English is so imprecise. Of course, we have written our charts; that's true. You will live out your chart whether you like it or not, because you wrote it; that's all true. But what you must know and what's so exciting is that there can be interference. We were under the assumption that God can't interfere.

We ascend to God. God doesn't descend to us; He can't. He is static, He is continuous; He is omnipotent and perfect. She, Mother God, rules the emotional side of this world. Whenever I get into a difficult issue with those I "mother," I say to Her, "Please help me because You know what it's like to be a mother." I pray to Her for things of this Earth. For things of spirituality, I pray to God the Father.

We are the emotional side of God.

The other night my oldest son, Paul, called me because his two prized Labradors were missing. To some people animals don't mean anything, but to my family, they mean everything, the same as people do. These are black hunting dogs, and he was just about hysterical. Empathizing with his pain of losing those dogs, I was frantic. I jumped in the car with him and went searching.

I said to him, "Paul, listen to me. If you quit screaming, crying, and banging the steering wheel, I will be able to help you." I've said that I'm not psychic with my family, but I think God grants special favors when in service to others. I don't know Almaden Valley (the area where he lives) at all, but I said, "Is there a street that starts with Red?"

He said, "Mom, there is a Redmond."

I said, "Turn left, then a quick right."

I had no idea where I was. All of a sudden, we found the dogs. While I'm doing this, though, I'm praying to my grandmother. But before I even prayed to my grandmother, I prayed to Azna. I don't know why Her name is Azna. Francine says that's what everyone calls Her. She's had so many names, I don't think She would mind if we called Her "Suzy-Q."

Dear Mother God,

We know that You are strong. We know that You rule this planet and all things physical within it. Today we petition You to give us the grace and the inspiration to meld ourselves with You, the Holy Spirit, and our Father in heaven. We ask that all people, and especially mothers, be healed in their hearts, their minds, and their souls. We ask that the power of You descend upon us and give our life new meaning. We ask that Your Mantle of Love be around us, that You and Your Gigantic Force and Omnipotence guide our lives, and that You help imbue us with the grace to heal and to help others. More important, after all these thousands of years to have come back to You—all these thousands of years that You have been ignored, pushed back, made fun of, thought to be a cult, secretive—that we now view You and unmask You and drop the veil that hides You, to once again, within our Gnostic religion, give You the power, the love, the honor that You so richly deserve. In doing so, we ascend ourselves to You to put You in Your Divine Power and give us the power we need to disperse Your message and Your love. We ask this in the name of the Father, the Mother, the Holy Spirit, and the God-Consciousness.

MEDITATION—THE TRINITY

Let us close our eyes and lift our minds and hearts to God the Father, and Azna the Blessed Mother Goddess Who comes down and help us with everything. Let us feel Her love and Her wings of warmth enfold us. The Dove of the Holy Spirit appears above our head, which is the symbol of Novus and our commitment to our belief and our God-Consciousness and to the life we chose. Ask God Almighty and Azna and the Holy Spirit and our God-Consciousness to rid us of all our negativity, to drop it and chip it away, that Azna's wings of hope and love and Divinity surround us and keep us protected.

Jesus said, "Mother, behold thy son. Son, behold thy Mother."

We say today, "Mother, behold thy child. Child, behold thy Mother."

I want you to take yourself to a beautiful Grecian-like temple and open the doors. Feel and sense and visualize that coming up from your right is Jesus—reddish-brown hair, large brown eyes, tall and slender, beautiful hands raised to touch you, a garment of white and purple, and a beautiful gold light around him.

In the middle of the temple is Azna, the Mother God. To the left of Her is our own Om, the Father God, and then our God-Consciousness, a beautiful beam of light. In the middle of this beautiful Trinity, a true Trinity, when Jesus touches us, we feel the infusion of health. Put all the names of your loved ones in the circle, put yourself in the middle of this, and put everyone else in the circle. From the top of the dome of this Grecian-columned building with the amber-stained glass, the light of the sun seems to move and rotate in the sky. It hits the amber light, the green light, the orange light, the blue light, the gold. It keeps rotating so that each one of these lights, like a kaleidoscope, fills our hearts, sanctifies our being, and above all, gives us the truth of our own conviction, whatever that may be, and the conviction of our intellect.

This religion won't be for the masses or those who do not utilize their full intelligence and think for themselves, totally on their own. That isn't being mean; it's a fact. People entrust their salvation to someone else. We want to earn our salvation and our own Divinity, lifting up toward God and touching part of Him. We feel sanctified, and we ask for our lives to be easier because we're on the right track. From this day forward, we ask that negativity not hit us—even if we must deal with it, it won't be part of us. We can deal with it as if we're looking through a Plexiglas covering. We ask this in the name of Mother God, Father God, Jesus, the Holy Spirit and our own God-Consciousness. Bring yourself up to yourself, feeling blessed, loved, protected, and full of grace.

MEDITATION—DESTROYING FEARS

Dear God, we ask for guidance, love, and your healing power for all the people who are close to us. We ask for special healing to be sent to all—to get through the next week with their trials, their tribulations, and their heartaches. We ask this in the name of the Holy Spirit and the Mother and Father God. We ask that each and every one of us, our family and our friends [quietly list the names of any people you wish], *will be joined together in this prayer for healing.*

Don't be afraid to ask for yourself. For anyone that's having financial worries and problems, anyone who is having job worries, love affair problems, marriage problems, ask that the grace of God flows so that the answers are available— and mostly that we don't get so burned out from life's toils and trials that we're not able to walk strong.

Feel a green light shooting through the very top of your head and moving down through your face, and down through your whole entire body. This emerald-green light that's healing spreads down even to your hands so that you will also be able to go out and heal others. Down through the whole trunk of the body into the lower half of the body, legs, clear down to the toes. Outside that, white and gold light.

I want you to think of yourself standing in a meadow, with the sun is shining on your face. You're standing there, and you're glowing with the White Light around you. I want you to begin to put out in front of you all your phobias, all your fears, all your worries, and I want you to label them like muddy dark blocks. Label them anxiety, money worries, love matters, and fears: fear of losing anything; fear of death; fear of annihilation; fear of not having a job that's good enough; fear of getting old and feeble; or whatever else it is that you fear.

I want you to take both of your hands, mentally, and put them in the White Light around you. I want you to pull that Light toward you and make it like a snowball. Throw that Light from your arm, from your emanation, toward those blocks of fears and worries. They begin to crumble and split. You reach your hands in again, and you take another ball of Light and throw it. You feel your strength and your God-Centeredness. Each time you throw this Light, the fear, worry, and anxiety crumble. Now they're all dissolved; all those fears, pains, and anxieties are gone. You're going to steal yourself away from them, and you're not going to start gathering new ones.

You're going to really open your arms wide, staying in that meadow, and say with all of your heart, all of your soul, "Thy will be done." God's will is your will. It's not different. Once you know that and you give it up to God, you will never have to be worried again. Really give it up, give it all up. Thy will be done. Bring yourself out on the count of three, all the way out. One, two, three . . .

BENEDICTION—GNOSTIC BLESSING

This is the truest form of sacrament, or sacred oath, used by the Gnostics at Qumran centuries ago. It's led by a minister and repeated by all.

Blessed Be God, The Father,
Blessed Be His Holy Name.
Blessed Be The Name of Azna,
Blessed Be Her Holy Name.
Blessed Be The Name Of Our Lord, Jesus Christ,
Blessed Be His Holy Name.
Blessed Be The Archetypes That Protect Us,
Blessed Be Their Holy Names.
Blessed Be Our Spirit Guides,

Blessed Be All Their Holy Names.
Blessed Be Everyone Here Today,
Blessed Be All Our Names.
Blessed Be Our Loved Ones Not Present,
Blessed Be All Their Names.
— Amen

ö ö ö

Arem, Shem, Beth, Sedal, Sacravelian, Ahad.
(*Translation:* "Blessed be this Queen on high
who is Sacred to all who come to Her. Amen.")

ö ö ö

NOVUS CELEBRATIONS

Spring Equinox
March 21—*The time of new beginnings.*

Blessing of the Children
May 30—*Annual Gnostic blessing for children.*

Summer Solstice
June 21—*The time in which all the faithful would bring gifts and coins in honor of benefits received.*

Festival of Lights
August 21—*A time of celebration for the early Gnostics who wanted to pay homage to the Mother Goddess, who was the symbol of human fertility, the Earth, and all growing things. Candles are a symbol of your soul.*

Autumn Equinox

September 21—*Not only the time of harvest, but the time of giving honor and homage to the Earth, which was the domain and dominion of the Mother Goddess.*

Mother Azna's Feast Day

December 8—*Our testimonial to our Blessed Mother, where we submit petitions and special prayers to Her.*

Winter Solstice

December 21—*This is the time of remembrance, of quiet and introspection for the year that has passed and the lessons we have learned. This is the time to bury all old pains and guilt and illnesses and fears under a white mantle of snow, which will purify deeds we have done or deeds done to us. In this way, it's a time of remembrance and a time of forgetting and forgiving.*

❦ About the Author ❦

Millions of people have witnessed **Sylvia Browne's** incredible psychic powers on TV shows such as *Montel Williams, Larry King Live, Entertainment Tonight,* and *Unsolved Mysteries;* she has also been profiled in *Cosmopolitan, People* magazine, and other national media. Her on-target psychic readings have helped police solve crimes, and she astounds audiences wherever she appears. Sylvia is the author of numerous books and tapes.

❦   ❦   ❦

Contact Sylvia Browne at:
www.sylvia.org

or

Sylvia Browne Corporation
35 Dillon Ave.
Campbell, CA 95008
(408) 379-7070

❦   ❦   ❦

Other Hay House Titles of Related Interest

BOOKS

Born to Be Together: *Love Relationships,*
Astrology, and the Soul,
by Terry Lamb

Colors & Numbers: *Your Personal Guide*
to Positive Vibrations in Daily Life,
by Louise L. Hay

The Experience of God:
How 40 Well-Known Seekers Encounter the Sacred,
edited by Jonathan Robinson

Experiencing the Soul: *Before Birth, During Life, After Death,*
by Eliot Jay Rosen

Infinite Self: *33 Steps to Reclaiming Your Inner Power,*
by Stuart Wilde

The Lightworker's Way:
Awakening Your Spiritual Power to Know and Heal,
by Doreen Virtue, Ph.D.

Magi Astrology™: *The Key to Success in Love and Money,*
by The Magi Society®

AUDIO PROGRAMS
Developing Your Own Psychic Powers, by John Edward

Psychic and Intuitive Healing,
by Barbara Brennan, Rosalyn Bruyère, and Judith Orloff, M.D.,
with Michael Toms

Unleashing Your Psychic Potential, by John Edward

Understanding Your Angels and Meeting Your Guides,
by John Edward

Notes

Notes

Notes

Notes

Notes

Notes

THIS IS THE NEWSLETTER YOU'VE BEEN WAITING FOR . . .

Find out SYLVIA BROWNE'S secrets for developing *your* psychic powers!

Order your subscription today to the *Sylvia Browne Newsletter*, and receive an exclusive lecture tape from Psychic Sylvia Browne—absolutely **FREE!**

Now is your chance to hear from your favorite author and psychic Sylvia Browne —six times a year—in the pages of this remarkable newsletter!

As a subscriber to the newsletter, you'll learn inside information directly from Sylvia Browne. You'll find out how to **connect with your angels,** learn about the **Other Side,** and get Sylvia's latest **predictions,** as well as information on how to **get and stay healthy.**

You'll be the first to hear about **the latest psychic discoveries** of Sylvia or her psychic son, **Chris Dufresne.** Also, your subscription allows you to **write to Sylvia** whenever you want, and as often as you like—and one of your questions may be featured in an upcoming newsletter along with Sylvia's answer.

Send for your Subscription and FREE lecture tape today!

IN A RUSH? Call **800-654-5126,** or fax postcard to **800-650-5115!**
www.hayhouse.com

Fold along dotted line.

Exclusive
SYLVIA BROWNE
Lecture Tape—FREE!

With one-year subscription